PRIVATE LESSONS

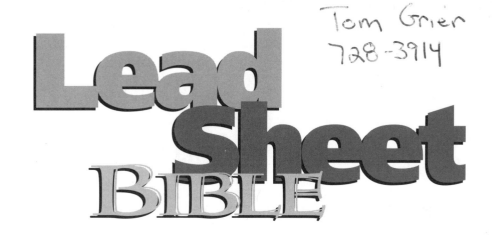

by Robin Randall
and Janice Peterson

D1462593

Illustrations by Jessica Lang

ISBN 0-7935-7127-8

7777 W. BLUEMOUND RD. P.O. BOX 13819 MILWAUKEE, WI 53213

Visit Hal Leonard Online at
www.halleonard.com

Acknowledgements

From Robin

Many people helped me during the long process of writing this book. First, a big thank–you to Paul LeWolt and Luke Hannington for doing and redoing the music graphics in the previous edition. Jack Smalley, Jerry Grant, and Terry Shaddick gave much appreciated advice and generously shared their musical knowledge, and Holland Mac Fallister donated "Surfboard Queen of Idaho," which set the tone of the book.

The following people also deserve my gratitude: Judithe Randall, Denise Gentilins, Diana De Witt, Reichart Von Wolfshield, David Pascal, Van Arno, Jessica Lang, Thair Peterson, James Butler, Craig Avery, Nancy Krasn, Steve Zell, Kelly Palmer, Ritch Esra, Debra Taub, Roberta Gunderson, Peter Knight at Global Music, Jeff Silverman, the folks at Valle Music and at Hollywood Sheet Music, the staff at the former Dick Grove School of Music and at the Musicians Institute—especially George DuBose, Jim McMains, Jeff Yock, Suzanne Saunders and Vocal Power. Added thanks to Guy ("with a D in the bass") Marshall.

Lastly, this book would not have been possible without my piano teacher of fifteen years, Guy Holtz, and my grandparents, Al and Mimi Schwartz, who supported my musical career every half step of the way. Thank you.

From Janice

My biggest thank-you goes to Robin, for talking me into helping her write a how-to music book. My husband, Dan, also deserves oodles of praise for patiently explaining Quark XPress to me, for letting me monopolize the computer, and for helping me to escape to Montana. Special thanks also to Paul LeWolt, Lisa, and Thair.

To Pops, thanks for trying to teach me the value of music, the sin of wordiness, and how to accept criticism—if not gracefully, at least with an open mind.

The following singers and producers graciously lent their talents to the audio that accompanies this book: Diana De Witt, Marcie Free, Aina Olsen, James Christian, Guy Marshall, Steve Hopkins, Tomie Reeves, Tony Sciuto, Holland Mac Fallister, Claude Gaudette, and Ron Wasserman.

Introduction

This book is for the average singer, songwriter, or musician who wants to create a lead sheet or chord chart that is easy to follow.

What Is a Lead Sheet?

A lead sheet is a simplified, streamlined form of sheet music that showcases a song's melody. Lead sheets typically include lyrics written below the melody and chord symbols written above.

Lead sheets capture the essence of a song—the melody, the harmony, and the lyrics—without getting bogged down by the exact details of the accompaniment—things like chord voicings, rhythms, instrumentation, and so on.

The virtues of the lead sheet are many. Because they are compact, lead sheets make a song easy to follow and therefore, easier to learn and memorize. Their brevity also makes lead sheets physically easier to handle than most other types of sheet music—a practical advantage for the performing musician. In addition, lead sheets are adaptable to any number of different musical situations or ensembles. What they lose in exactness, they more than make up for in freedom and possibility. They are an ideal way to notate looser, more improvisational forms of music such as pop, rock, blues, and jazz.

What Is a Chord Chart?

A chord chart is essentially a lead sheet in reverse—a showcase for a song's accompaniment. The typical chord chart is made up of chords symbols and slashes, with word cues inserted below the staff to help musicians keep their place in the song.

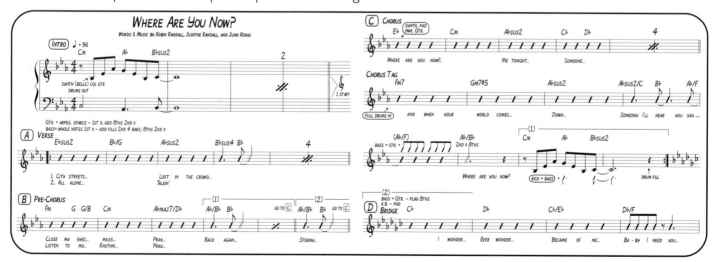

Chord charts are useful in situations where a rhythm section or accompanist must back up a lead singer or instrumentalist. They are great for doing demos and showcases.

How to Use This Book

This book can be broken down into roughly three sections:

Ch. 1-4   Lead sheet writing is about communication. Before we can communicate music, we must first understand its concepts and notation, so these chapters focus on the language and grammar of music—notes, intervals, scales, keys, chords, and rhythm. They are chock full of examples that will sharpen your mind and ear.

Ch. 5-8   These next four chapters introduce matters more directly related to lead sheet writing: song form, road maps, transposition, and how to notate accompaniment. These essential tools will give you a jump start on the final section of the book.

Ch. 9-11   If you're currently thinking of writing a lead sheet, chances are you've either composed an original song, heard a recording you'd like to transcribe, or have sheet music for a song that just doesn't suit your performance needs. In this section, we'll address each one of these situations individually. In fact, we'll follow three different paths:

sheet music   →   chord chart

original song   →   Lead sheet

recording   →   chord chart

To help us through the process, we'll meet three characters—Brandi, Barry, and Bo. Each has a different challenge to meet. We'll learn along with them how to write lead sheets and chord charts, using their songs as our examples.

Recommended Materials

All you really need to get started with this book is a pencil and staff paper; however, if you intend to get serious about writing lead sheets and chord charts, I do suggest you seek out the following items:

- Tape recorder (with pitch control)
- Musical instrument
- Staff paper
- Ruler
- Pencils (#2)
- Eraser
- Ballpoint pen
- Calligraphy pens—medium and fine-tip (2.5 mm. and 1.5 mm.)
- Black markers (medium and fine-line)
- Highlighter
- Liquid Paper/Whiteout (one for pen and ink; one for copies)
- Staff line correction strips (found at music supply stores)
- Colored pencils (two different colors)
- White correction tape (1 line, 2 line, and 6 line)
- Stencil, a rubber stamp kit, or rub-on letters (for song titles)

NOTE: Many professional copyists believe that only fountain pens and black ink should be used on final copy, but I think a felt tip pen is more practical, especially for beginners.

Prologue: Brandi's Audition

"Next!"

A humorless-looking man peered from around the door. Brandi clutched her sheet music and started forward. She followed the little man through the door and down the long hallway, past the "'Celebrity Search' Auditions-This Way" sign. She couldn't believe that she was finally here: "Toto, we're not in Kansas anymore." The man looked at her. She realized she had said this aloud. "Oh… I'm not actually from Kansas. I'm from Idaho… Boise, Idaho… you know… potatoes." He said nothing; he kept walking.

She babbled on: "L.A.'s sooooo big, and I've even learned how to surf! But that's not why I came, of course. I really came to audition for 'Celebrity Search.' Imagine… $100,000 and maybe a record deal!"

They came to a well-lit rehearsal hall. At one end, at a long table, were three more humorless faces—two producers and a musical director. At the other end of the hall was a stage with a piano player, bright lights, and a video camera. Her expressionless guide pointed her toward the stage.

"Name!" a voice commanded from the dark.

"Brandi… well, Barbra… but Brandi."

"Well? Which is it?" the voice asked impatiently. **"Barbara or Brandi?"**

"Well, my real name is Barbra… that's B-A-R-B-R-A. But my friends call me 'Brandi.' You know… like the song? My mom went into labor when that song was a hit and…"

"Barbra or Brandi?"

"Brandi."

"Thank you! Now please talk over your music with the piano player."

Brandi walked over to the piano and started to place her music, sheet by sheet, in front of the piano player, who asked her how many pages she had.

"Eight," Brandi answered, carefully layering her sheets. "No… six." She quickly grabbed the two sheets from the floor and put them back on the piano.

He looked at her amused. "You want me to play the song in *this* order?"

"Uh… no… uh…" She shuffled the pages, then realized they wouldn't all fit on the piano stand.

"Tape?" he offered.

"Yeah… great idea."

She'd only taped two pages together when the voice from the dark asked, **"Can we *please* pick up the pace?"**

"Yes, I'm sorry… right away." She quickly taped the remaining pages in order and placed them on the piano.

The piano player looked at her. She looked at him. She wondered why he didn't start playing and why he continued to look at her. "So?" she asked, puzzled.

"So…" he said, mimicking her, "what's the tempo? Count it off."

"Oh, OK. One… two… one……… two… three… four………"

"Wait, wait, wait… You gotta be consistent. I can't get the feel of the song. Why don't you sing the song in your head first, and then count the tempo out loud to me."

Brandi hummed a few bars of the melody and this time counted correctly. The piano player started playing. Brandi sang the first line, then stopped.

"What's the matter now?" he asked.

"The key. It's too low. I can't sing in this key!"

"You didn't know this before?"

"Well, no… I thought it'd be just like the record."

"Well, it's not."

"Is there a problem, Brandi?"

"Uh… no…"

The piano player stepped in. "I have to transpose the song for her."

"We don't have time for this. Why don't we reschedule Brandi for *next* week, and she can transpose her own song before then."

"Okay… thank you… I'm sorry. I'll see you next week."

"You know," said the piano player, "all I really need is a chord chart. You already know the melody. A chord chart would have fewer pages and wouldn't fall off the piano. You can hire someone to write out the chords."

"But that costs a lot, and I don't have any money right now."

"Well, you could do it yourself."

"Yeah, right."

"It's not that hard. I have a book you can use."

"A book? I'll never finish it by next week."

"You can't *read?*"

"Of course I can read, but I can't finish a book *and* write a chord chart by next week."

"Sure you can. It's a guide; it's step-by-step. You can write the chart as you go along. It's easy. What have you got to lose?"

"Nothing, I guess."

AHEM… IS THERE A PROBLEM… BRANDI?

Chapter One
THE BASICS

For those who don't already read or notate music, a crash course in these basic terms and concepts is necessary in order to begin creating lead sheets and chord charts.

Staff and Clef

Notes are typically placed on a staff made up of five lines and four spaces. A *clef* sign is placed on the far left of a staff. The two most commonly used clefs are the *treble clef* and the *bass clef*:

The treble clef is used for music in the high registers—female voice, male tenor voice, right hand of the piano, and guitar; the bass clef is used for music in the low registers—bass, left hand of the piano, and some drum parts.

Notes

The clef sign determines the names of the notes, which follow the first seven letters of the alphabet—A, B, C, D, E, F, and G. Notes on the lines for each clef are as follows:

Notes in the spaces are:

In the treble clef, when the notes on the lines and the note in the spaces are combined, the staff looks like this:

In the bass clef, when the notes on the lines and spaces are combined, the staff looks like this:

Together, the two clefs form what is called a *grand staff:*

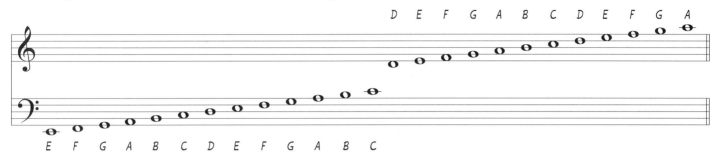

Ledger Lines

Additional lines above or below a staff are called *ledger lines.* These increase the range of a clef.

Ledger lines should be drawn approximately one quarter of an inch long and parallel to the staff. The lines should be thin, so as not to obscure the notehead. Spacing between ledger lines and the staff should be even, of equal distance. When several adjacent notes have ledger lines, all of them should line up.

Half Steps and Whole Steps

Half steps and whole steps are a way of measuring the distance, or *interval,* between two notes. The shortest possible distance between two notes on a piano is a *half step.* Two half steps equal one *whole step.*

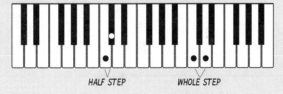

HALF STEP   WHOLE STEP

Sharps and Flats

Sharps and flats can be used to create half steps and whole steps from any note.

Sharp (♯)
Raises a note a half step

Double sharp (𝄪)
Raises a note one whole step

Flat (♭)
Lowers a note a half step

Double flat (♭♭)
Lowers a note one whole step

Natural (♮)
Restores a note to its original pitch

Notice that the same note on a piano can be spelled multiple ways—as a sharped or a flatted note—depending on the direction from which it is approached. Such note pairs as C# and D♭ are said to be *enharmonic equivalents*—two note names for the same pitch. Which spelling is chosen depends on the harmonic context or on personal preference.

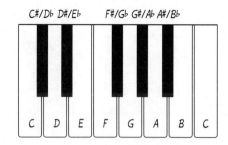

Noteheads, Stems, and Flags

Note durations are indicated by the use of noteheads, stems, and flags.

Noteheads should be drawn slightly egg-shaped and all the same size. If a notehead is placed in a space on the staff, it should be drawn large enough to be easily recognized, but not so large that it intrudes onto the adjoining line or space. Stay within two staff lines and be sure to close the notehead-don't draw a partial notehead. Similar rules apply for noteheads drawn on a line; they must be easy to see, but not too large or thick.

Correct   Incorrect

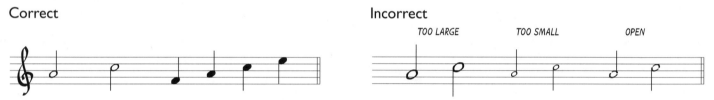

Stems go up on notes that fall below the middle line (the B note on the treble clef; D note on the bass). They go down on notes that fall on or above the middle line.

Stems that go down are attached to the left side of the notehead. Stems that go up attach to the right side of the notehead.

Correct   Incorrect

Stem length is approximately one octave above the notehead if the stem is going up and one octave below the notehead if the stem is going down. Stems must connect to noteheads—don't leave a space—and should be drawn straight and thin. The "vertical" edge of a slanted felt-tip pen works well for this.

A single stem should connect all the notes of a chord. Stem direction is determined by the lowest or highest note in the chord, relative to the middle line of the staff.

A curved line attached to the top or bottom of a stem is called a *flag*. A single flag identifies an eighth note, a double flag identifies a sixteenth note, and a triple flag identifies a thirty-second note. A flag curves down on stems that go up and curves up on stems that go down. Flags are always attached to the right side of the stem and are drawn from top to bottom.

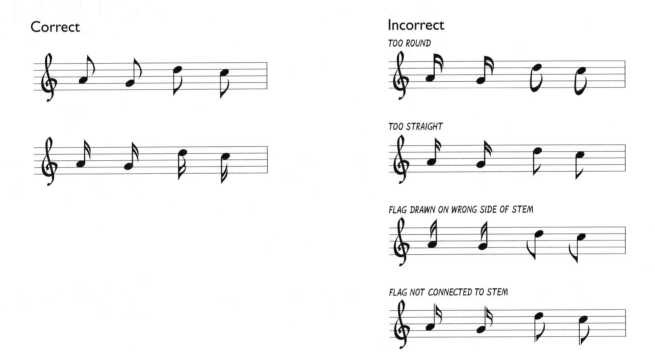

Chapter Two

2 SCALES, KEYS, & ACCIDENTALS

Scale and key are concepts that, by putting notes into a larger perspective, help us to make sense of a piece of music. A firm understanding of them is invaluable for writing, transcribing, and even memorizing music.

Major Scales

Remember half steps and whole steps? A *scale* is really nothing but a series of whole and half steps in a particular set pattern. Below is a major scale starting on a C. Notice the pattern of whole and half steps that it follows.

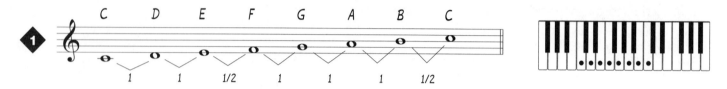

The above pattern—whole, whole, half, whole, whole, whole, half—is *the* pattern that defines a major scale. It can be applied to any of the twelve notes within the octave for a total of twelve possible major scales.

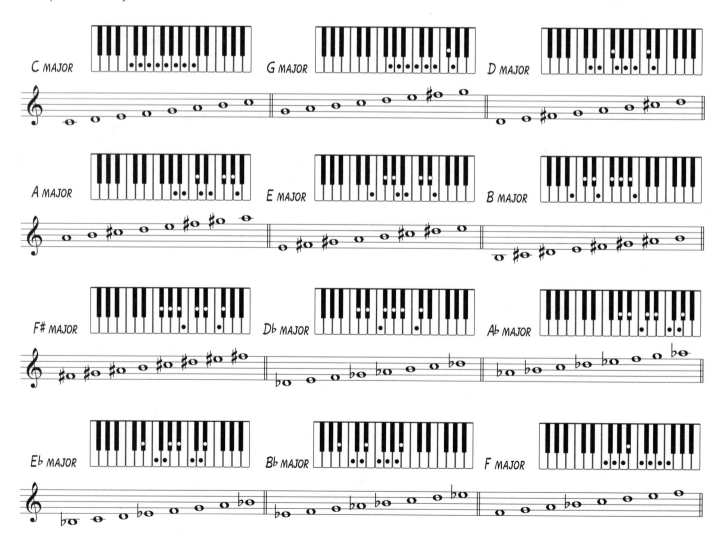

When building a scale, notes should appear in order and all note names should be accounted for. Two of the examples below are correct and two are incorrect. Notice the difference.

Correct   Incorrect

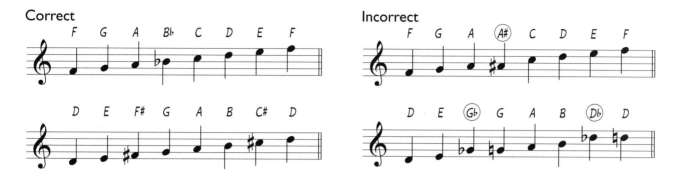

Minor Scales

Every major key has a relative minor, and though there is just one major scale, there are actually three varieties of minor scale: natural, harmonic, and melodic. Each is defined below, followed by an appropriate example in the key of A minor (the relative minor of C major). Notice how the whole- and half-step patterns change with each type.

A *natural minor* scale has the same notes as its relative major but starts on the 6th degree of that scale.

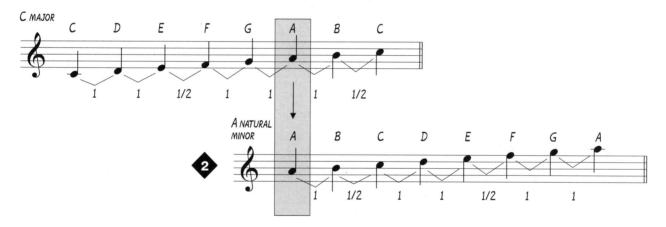

A *harmonic minor* scale has the same notes as the natural minor, but the 7th degree is raised a half step.

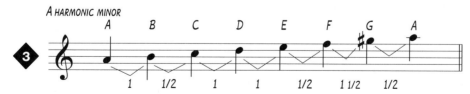

A *melodic minor* scale has the same notes as the natural minor, but the 6th and 7th degrees are raised a half step when ascending and then naturalized when descending the scale.

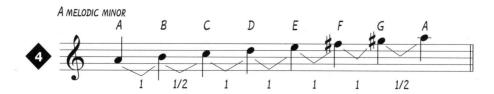

Pentatonic and Blues Scales

The following three scales are variations on the basic major and minor scales learned above. You should learn to recognize them because they are extremely common in pop, rock 'n' roll, R&B, Motown, gospel, and country music.

A *major pentatonic* scale is a five-note scale with the same notes as a major scale, but with the 4th and 7th degrees deleted.

A *minor pentatonic* scale is a five-note scale with the same notes as a natural minor scale, but with the 2nd and 6th degrees deleted.

A *blues scale* is a six-note scale with the same notes as a minor pentatonic scale, but with a flatted 5th degree added.

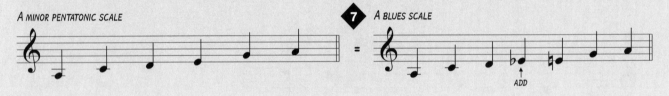

Key Signatures

The more you work with scales and keys other than C major or A minor, the more you'll realize the value of key signatures. A *key signature*, placed at the start of every staff (immediately after the clef) tells a musician how many sharps or flats a piece of music contains.

Sharps or flats appearing in a key signature affect all of the notes of that particular name, wherever those notes may occur on the staff or in the music. For example, if a lead sheet has a key signature of F major—which has one flat, B♭—all of the B notes in the lead sheet are flatted. By marking a key signature of F major, none of the subsequent B notes need to be marked with the flat symbol. This saves the lead sheet writer from having to notate every sharp or flat as it occurs:

For every major and minor scale, there is a corresponding major and minor key. The same key signature is used to refer to both a major key and its relative minor.

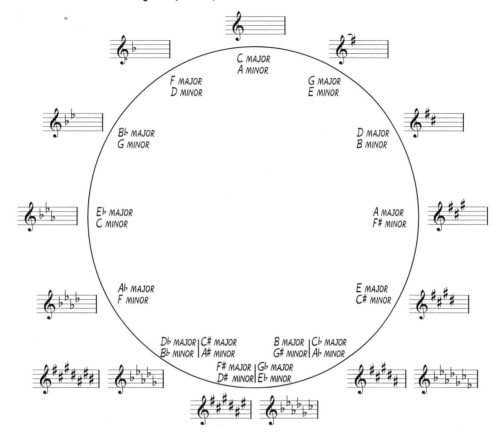

Notice that the number of flats or sharps in a key signature can range from zero to seven (because there are seven note names—A, B, C, D, E, F, and G—to be sharped or flatted) and that the sharps or flats appear in a set order.

Interestingly, the order of the flats…   B - E - A - D - G - C - F

is the reverse of the order of the sharps.   F - C - G - D - A - E - B

Accidentals

In addition to the sharps or flats found in a key signature, other sharps or flats may occur in a piece of music if the melody ventures outside of the indicated key. Sharps and flats not appearing in the key signature are called **accidentals**; they temporarily raise or lower a pitch or restore it to its normal state. Accidentals should be written directly in front of the note they affect. If the note is written on the line, the accidental is also written on the line; if the note is in a space, the accidental is written in the space.

Accidentals remain in effect for the full length of the measure in which they appear. For example, if there are three C♯s in a single measure, only the first needs to be preceded with a sharp (♯) sign. If the following measure contains a C♯, however the sharp sign (♯) must be reindicated.

Conversely, if a measure contains one C# followed by two C naturals, the second of the three Cs should be preceded by a natural (♮), sign in order to cancel the previous sharp.

Courtesy Accidentals and Key Changes

Technically, an accidental only affects the note and the measure in which it appears; however, it's common practice to cancel accidentals in different octaves of the same measure or in the same octave of the next measure, if they are no longer in effect.

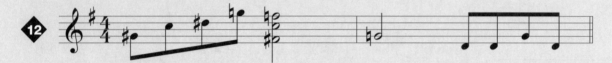

Such accidentals are termed *courtesy accidentals* because they are a courtesy to the performing musician. By erasing any potential doubt about the intended pitch, they make your lead sheet easier to read.

A somewhat similar practice is adopted for changes of key signature. In cases where a key change would occur at the beginning of a new staff line, advance notice is given at the *end of the previous staff,* to signal the coming change. Again, this is a courtesy to the performing musician.

If You Remember Love

By Jeff Law, Judithe & Robin Randall

Chapter Three
RHYTHM

The basic elements of music are sound and time. Sound organized in real time is *rhythm*—a series of patterned beats or pulsations. A ticking clock, a heartbeat, a pulse—all are examples of rhythm. In many ways, time and rhythm could be considered the "canvas" of a song; they provide the backdrop to which the notes, chords, and melody—the "colors"—are added.

Note Durations

Note durations begin with the whole note and then subdivide by two into halves, quarters, eighths, sixteenths, and so on. Every note value has a corresponding value in silence, called a *rest.*

A note's duration can be prolonged by the use of a dot or a tie. A *dot* placed after a note (or rest) adds to the note one-half of its rhythmic value.

For notes in spaces, the dot is placed in the center of the space, directly after the notehead. For notes on the lines, the dot is placed in the center of the space *above* the note.

A *tie* placed after a note prolongs it by any desired rhythmic value. When two notes are tied, only the first is struck; the second note represents the duration that the first note should be sustained.

A tie should not to be confused with a *slur,* which indicates that one syllable of a lyric is drawn out over two or more melody notes, or that a melodic phrase should be played or sung smoothly without separating the notes.

A slur encompasses all tones of a small melodic unit, such as a phrase, half-phrase, or motif. When the stems of the notes go up, the slur is written underneath the notes. When the stems go down, the slur is written above the notes.

Meter

Most people feel beats in patterns of two, three, or four. The pattern into which a stream of beats is divided is called *meter*. The marching command "Hup, two, three, four" would be a prime example of a four-beat pattern or meter. The "tick-tock" of a clock would be an example of a two-beat meter. In this latter example, the first beat ("tick") is stressed or accented and is referred to as the *downbeat*, while the second beat ("tock") receives less stress and is referred to as the *upbeat*.

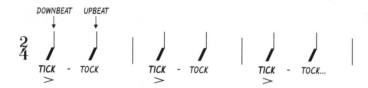

Meter is expressed in music notation by the use of *measures*, or bars, which represent the time interval from one primary downbeat to the next, and by *time signatures*, which indicate the number of beats in each measure.

Generally speaking, the top number of a time signature designates the number of beats, or counts, per measure, while the bottom number designates the note duration that receives a beat or count. In the above example in 4/4 for instance, each bar contains four beats, and each beat is represented by a quarter note; the quarter note is said to be the *beat unit*.

Simple vs. Compound Time

Any note duration can serve as a beat unit, but the quarter note is perhaps the most common because it can be easily subdivided into smaller note values, like eighths and sixteenths, or extended into larger ones, like halves and wholes. The second most common beat unit, as you can see from the table below, is the dotted quarter, which is useful for melodies in which the beat subdivides into three.

Meters in which the beat unit is divisible by two—like 2/4, 3/4, and 4/4—are called "simple" meters. Meters where the beat is divisible by three—like 6/8, 9/8, and 12/8—are called "compound." The important thing is not the terminology, but to be able to recognize the beat unit in a meter and to convey it consistently in your notation, from note spacing and beaming to choice of dotted vs. tied note values.

Spacing Beats within a Bar

Beats must be spaced evenly within a bar of music. For example, if you are writing a lead sheet in 4/4 time, the four beats in a typical bar should be spaced like this:

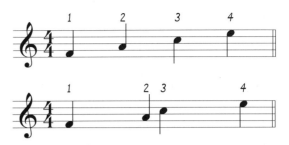

Do not space beats this way:

Even though the notation in the second example adds up to four beats, the spacing of the beats will confuse and frustrate the musician.

Don't Hide Beat 3

In 4/4 time, the first beat is the primary beat or down-beat, but the *third* beat is also important. It is a *secondary accented beat*. Not as strong as the first beat, it is never-theless stronger than the second and fourth beats.

When notating rhythms in 4/4 time, don't "hide" beat 3. It is difficult for a musician to subdivide a rhythm pattern when this basic beat structure of the meter is not shown clearly. Below are examples of melodies. Some show the downbeat of beat 3 by using ties across the imaginary line, the others hide beat 3.

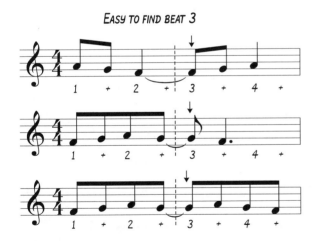

Both notations would sound identical when played; however, the examples on the left are easier for a musician to execute.

This "Don't hide beat 3" rule applies to rests also:

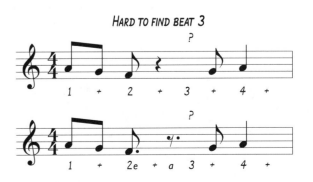

Even though a half rest can be placed on the second beat of a measure to indicate two beats of silence between two quarter notes, most musicians prefer to see quarter rests on beats 2 and 3:

There is one exception to the rule. It is OK not to show beat 3 when a "white note" (whole, half, or dotted half note) runs through the beat.

Note, however, that the half note must fall on a downbeat. A half note that falls on an upbeat is confusing; it makes it harder to find beat 2 and then buries beat 3.

Correct   Incorrect

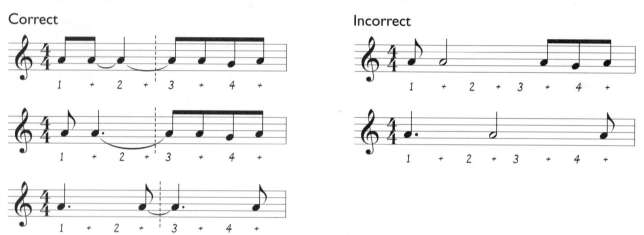

Beaming

When two or more flagged notes occur within a single beat unit, a **beam** is drawn to connect the notes and eliminate the flags. The first beam, or **primary beam**, connects eighth notes, while additional beams, called **secondary beams**, connect sixteenth notes. Both can be used in eighth- and sixteenth-note combinations.

In syncopated or dotted eighth- and sixteenth-note combinations, a **partial beam** must be used to distinguish the sixteenth note from the eighth note. This secondary beam always turns inward within its own group.

Always show the beat when beaming notes together—particularly when notating combinations of eighth and sixteenth notes. In other words, only beam together those notes that belong to a single beat unit.

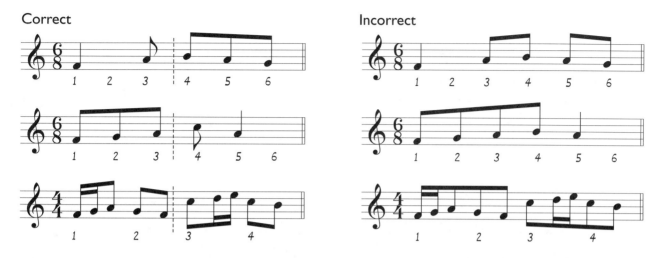

The one exception to this rule is in 4/4 time. If a measure or half-measure consists of only eighth notes, you can and should beam those notes together to highlight beat 3.

Beam and Stem Direction

The direction of beams and of stems in a beamed group is not arbitrary. The beam follows the direction of the notes within the group, when there is one. If a group of beamed notes sits above the middle staff line, the stems go down:

If the notes fall below the middle staff line, the stems go up:

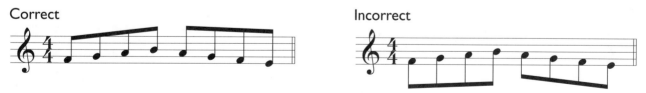

If notes sit both above and below the middle staff line, stem direction is determined by the highest or lowest note in the beamed group:

An exception to the stem direction rule occurs when there are two different melody lines on a single staff, to indicate separate verse melodies or additional harmonies behind the lead vocal. In these cases, the lead vocal or first verse should be stemmed in one direction, and the harmony or second verse should be stemmed in the opposite direction.

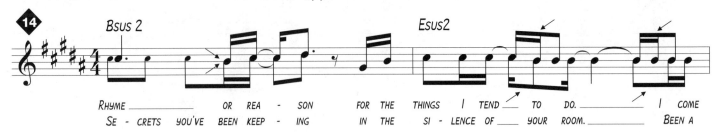

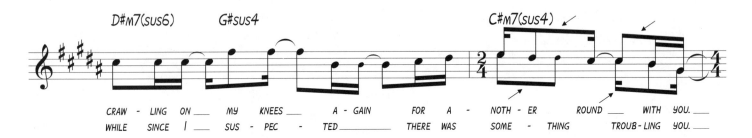

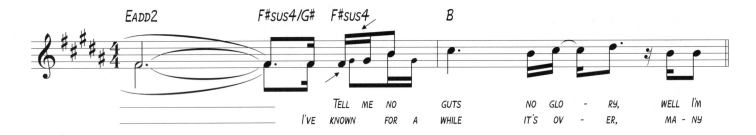

Counting Subdivisions

When two notes of equal time value take place in a single beat, the second is usually counted "and." This distinguishes the downbeats from the upbeats and stops a person counting from stretching out the notes: "Wuh-un… too-oo… three-ee… foh-or." "One-and-two-and-three-and-four-and" divides the quarter-note pulse into eighth notes. The downbeats are numbers and the upbeats are "and"s.

When dividing eighths into sixteenths, there are several ways to count the subdivisions. "One-ee-and-uh" and "one-ta-and-ta" are two popular choices. Whichever way is used, the goal is to subdivide quarter notes into four distinct parts.

Triplets and "Shuffle" Rhythm

A quarter note divided into two equal parts is represented as two eighth notes. A quarter note divided into *three* equal parts is notated as an eighth-note *triplet*.

Triplet rhythms can be counted off a number of ways. "One-la-lee, two-la-lee…," "one-ta-da, two-ta-da…," and "tri-pi-let, tri-pi-let…" are some common methods. Any note value can be divided into a triplet. If the triplet is a beamed note group, it can be indicated by placing a "3" above the beam. If the triplet is a larger, non-beamed note group (or broken-beamed), the "3" should be accompanied by a bracket.

Triplets form the basis of "shuffle rhythm," commonly found in the big band ("swing") music of the '40s and the early rock 'n' roll and blues music of the '50s. Shuffle rhythm can be derived from a triplet rhythm by combining the first two eighth notes of the triplet into a quarter. The result is like a triplet with a silent middle eighth note.

This shuffle notation can be hard to read though. So instead, use straight eighth notes with the word "swing" and (♫ = ♩♪) written at the beginning of the lead sheet or chord chart. This tells the musician to swing all eighth notes.

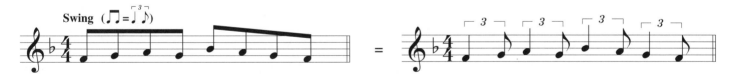

Syncopation

To *syncopate* a rhythm is to deliberately upset the normal or expected pattern of accents or meter. Syncopation shifts the accents in a measure from a strong beat to a weak beat or from a downbeat to an upbeat. It is frequently created by tying a weak beat or upbeat into the next strong beat or downbeat:

It can also be created by resting on a strong beat or downbeat:

Chapter Four

4 INTERVALS AND CHORDS

If melody is like the foreground of a painting, then chords are like the "background." Major chords function like bright colors; they lighten a song. Minor chords act like darker colors, adding a somber tone. A single melody harmonized with major chords can sound upbeat, while harmonized with minor chords, can sound sad.

It is important to be able to differentiate the various chord qualities (major, minor, dominant, etc.) and to know how to build them. Knowing how to identify and build chords gives you a better understanding of what musicians see and helps you communicate how you want a tune played. Also, sheet music often has inaccurate or insufficient chord symbols that must be corrected.

19 "Major" melody

"Minor" melody

Intervals

Intervals are the building blocks of chords. As we've already seen, one way to measure intervals is with whole steps and half steps, as on a piano. More commonly, intervals are labeled by *number* and *quality*.

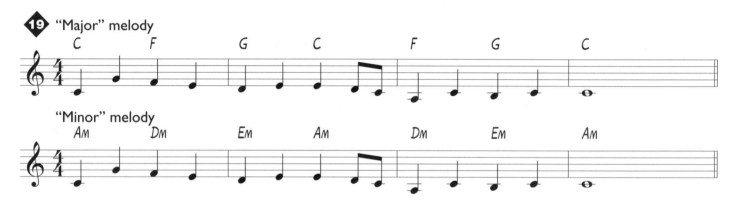

INTERVAL:	P1	m2	M2	m3	M3	P4	A4	D5	P5	m6	M6	m7	M7	P8
STEPS:	0	1/2	1	1 1/2	2	2 1/2		3	3 1/2	4	4 1/2	5	5 1/2	6

The number of each interval above can be verified by counting the lines and spaces between the two notes of the interval—or by relating those two notes to the degrees of a major scale. The qualities (major, minor, perfect, augmented, and diminished) are a matter of knowing the half and whole step equivalencies or of recognizing the distinctive aural properties of each.

Perfect Intervals

Only certain intervals can be labeled "perfect": unisons, 4ths, 5ths, and octaves. These are the intervals traditionally thought to be the most *consonant*—the most stable and resolved. They tend to have a hollow, open sound, and they occur naturally within both major and minor scales.

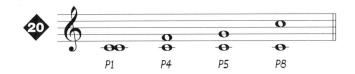

Major and Minor Intervals

2nds, 3rds, 6ths, and 7ths can be either major or minor. In general, 3rds and 6ths are considered more consonant than 2nds and 7ths, and major intervals are more *consonant* than minor ones. Major intervals tend to have a warm sound, while minor intervals often sound sad or distressful.

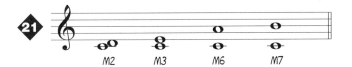
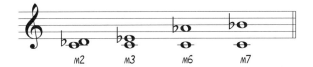

Any major interval can be made minor by decreasing its size just a half step—either raising the bottom note, or lowering the top note. Any minor interval can be made major by reversing this procedure.

Augmented and Diminished Intervals

Augmented and diminished intervals are generally considered the most *dissonant* of all intervals. They create a sense of tension, stress, urgency, or anxiety. The *tritone*—the diminished 5th or augmented 4th—is the defining interval of this type; it occurs naturally between the 7th and 4th degrees of a major scale.

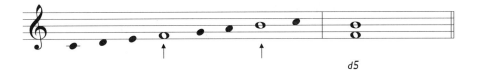

Any perfect interval can be made augmented by increasing its size one half step or made diminished by decreasing its size one half step.

Similarly, any major interval can be augmented, and any minor interval can be diminished, but the resulting interval will always be enharmonically equivalent to another, more common interval.

Triads

The simplest chord to build is a *triad*, which consists of just three notes stacked in intervals of a third. Scalewise, a triad is built from the root to the 3rd and from the 3rd to the 5th. There are four types of triads—what distinguishes each is the quality of its two component thirds.

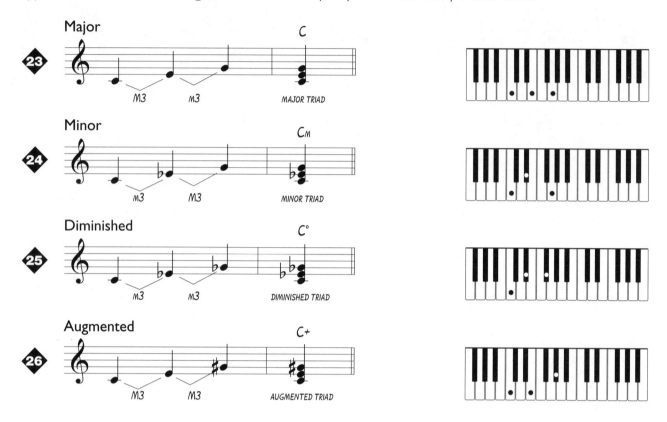

Seventh Chords

A 7th can be added to any triad to form a four-note chord called a *seventh chord.* There are two types of 7ths that can be added to a triad: a *major 7th,* which is a half step below the octave above the root of a major scale; and a *minor 7th,* which is a whole step below the octave above the root.

The 7th can also be seen as another 3rd stacked on top of the original triad. Based upon the original triad and the type of 7th that is added to it, there are several distinct types of seventh chords:

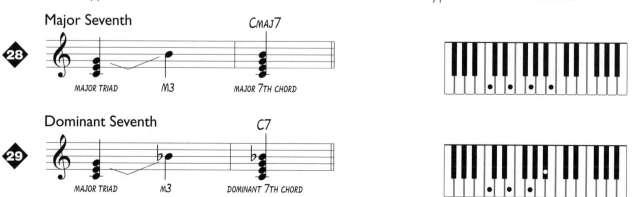

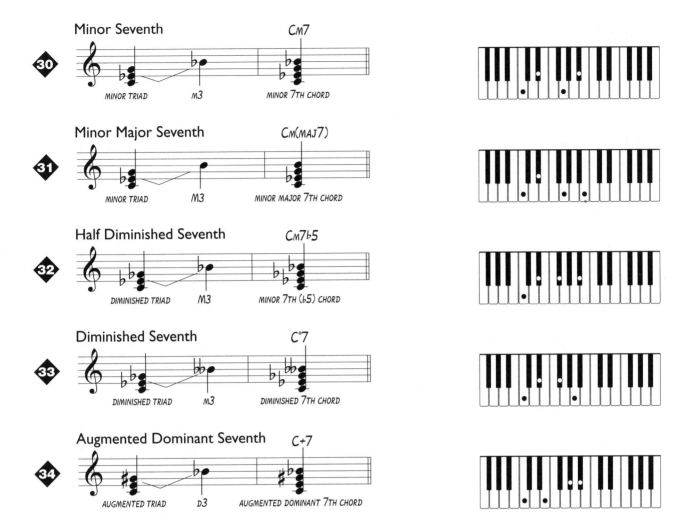

Extended Chords

It's quite possible to continue stacking thirds to produce more elaborate, *extended* chords—like ninths, elevenths, and thirteenths.

These chords, however, are generally not necessary for effective lead sheet writing. They are usually

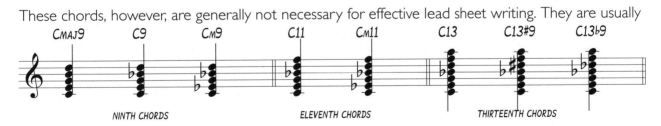

substitute chords, and their individual qualities can almost always be traced back to the particular seventh chord—major, dominant, minor, etc.—for which they substitute. If your lead sheet is intended to be played in a jazz style, just indicate this with a style description, and an experienced player will naturally substitute extended chords where appropriate.

Suspended and Add9 Chords

Triads can also be altered to create other kinds of chords, such as *suspended* and *add9* chords.

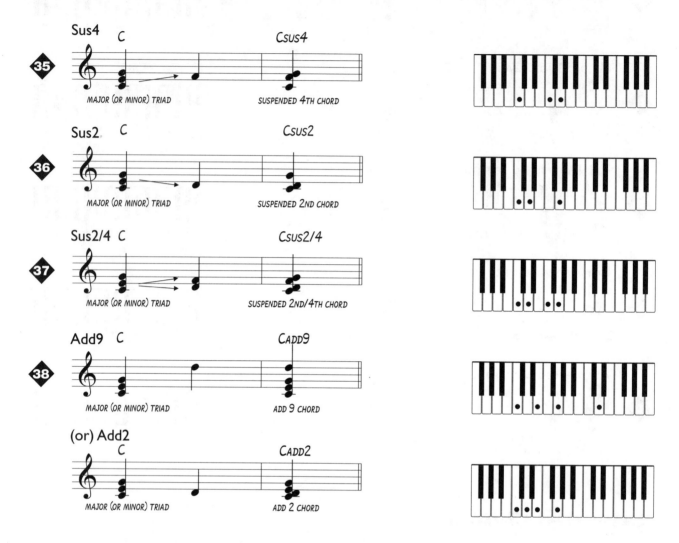

Sixth Chords

A *sixth chord* is created by adding a 6th to a major or minor triad. This is the equivalent of stacking a major 2nd on top of the chord.

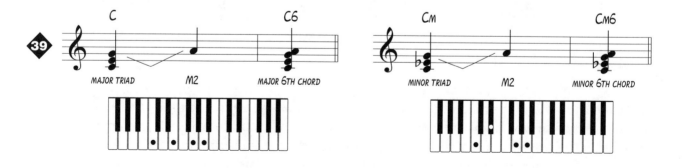

Power Chords

If the 3rd of a triad is *removed,* the result is a root-fifth dyad commonly called a *power chord.*

Technically speaking, the power chord isn't a true chord, because it consists of only two notes—the root and 5th of a triad. However, this root-5th dyad is so strong and stable, particularly when voiced on the lower strings of a guitar, for instance, that it implies a full chord. The power chord is particularly popular in rock music because it is easy to play and has a powerful, open sound. The absence of the 3rd degree, which normally determines whether a chord is major or minor, gives the chord its empty sound.

Chord Voicings

Generally, it is not necessary to notate specific chord voicings in a lead sheet or chord chart; most musicians can simply read the chord symbols and make up their own voicings. However, if you want a chord to sound exactly as it does in the recording, then it's worthwhile knowing some basic concepts of chord voicing.

Inversion refers to the order in which chord tones are stacked in a voicing—in particular, which chord tone is in the bass: root, 3rd, 5th, or 7th. A three-part chord has three possible positions; a four-part chord has four.

Open and *closed* refer to the spacing of chord tones within a voicing. In a *closed* voicing, chord tones appear in their tightest possible arrangement. In an *open* voicing, the tones are spread apart.

Doubling refers to the use of a chord tone (root, 3rd, 5th, etc.) in more than one octave within a voicing. The most commonly doubled chord tone is the root, because it tends to strengthen the tonality of a chord.

Slash Chords

A quick and easy way to notate inversions is with *slash chords*. In a slash chord, the bass note is indicated to the right of the regular chord symbol, after a slash mark. The slash chord C/E, for example, indicates that a C chord should be played with an E in the bass. This E could be played in the left hand of a piano part, as the bottom note of a guitar chord, or by the bass player.

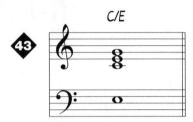 

Slash chords are generally only necessary if the note in the bass is particularly important—if it belongs to a descending bass line, for instance—or if the note does not normally belong in the chord and is necessary for the overall sound. C/F#, for instance, would be a *polychord* that contains a bass note not otherwise belonging to the chord.

Dos and Don'ts

When writing chord symbols, it's important to use the right words and signs, so as not to confuse the musician. Observe the following guidelines when labeling chords, and rely on the list of chord symbols below as your reference:

- The letter name of a chord symbol (e.g., C, Dm, Amaj7♭5) should always be capitalized.

- Major triads should be called by their letter name only. Do not, for instance, label a C major triad as "Cmaj"—this suggests a chord larger than a triad.

- Write "maj" when referring to major 7ths or other major chords larger than a triad.

- Do not use △ to refer to a major 7th chord; this is an informal, slang symbol.

- Do not cross 7s, because a 7 is sometimes used to symbolize a major 7th chord. A musician might misinterpret a crossed 7 as a major 7th chord when it is intended to be a dominant 7th.

- Write "m" when referring to a minor chord.

C	C7	Cm7	Cmaj7	Cadd6	Cm7#5(♭9)	Cm	C9
Cm9	Cmaj9	Cadd9	C7#5(♭9)	C°	C11	Cm11	C$^6_9$
Cadd4	C13sus4	C5	C7sus4	Cm7sus4	C/E	Cm(add4)	C7$^{#9}_{#5}$
C6	C9sus4	Cm(maj7)	Csus4	Cm(add9)	C13#9	Cm6	C7♭5
Cm$^6_9$	Csus2	Cm(add6)	C13♭9	C°7	C7♭9	Cm7♭5	C7#11
Cm(add$^6_9$)	C9#9	C+7	C7#9	C9#11	Csus$^2_4$	C9♭5	C7(no 3rd)

Chapter Five
5 SONG FORM

I f you know the *form*, or pattern, of a song, you know which sections repeat, which don't, and in what order they occur. You also know which sections need to be written out and which can be referred to with time-saving symbols such as repeat brackets. Form gives a song continuity, structure, and a recognizable quality. It's probably one of the first things you notice as a listener, and it should be one of the first things you take note of as a lead sheet writer.

Common Song Forms

Songs are typically made up of verses, choruses, and/or bridges—some or all of which may repeat. A quick and easy way to conceptualize a song is to assign a letter (A, B, C, etc.) to each distinct section of the song, then note when these sections recur. The two most common song forms are indicated this way below:

AABA: Verse, Verse, Bridge, Verse

ABAB: Verse, Chorus, Verse, Chorus

The AABA pattern is an older song form often found in early Broadway and vaudeville songs, as well as in many jazz standards and country songs. ABAB is found more often in contemporary music—particularly songs written after 1960, beginning with Motown and the British Invasion.

Variations on the above two forms are very common:

ABABCB: This is ABAB with a Bridge and Chorus added.

ABABCAB: This is ABAB with a Bridge, Verse, and Chorus added.

AABABA: This is AABA with the Bridge and Verse repeated.

AAA: This is AABA with the Bridge removed.

While the AAA song form may appear monotonous because the same musical verse is repeated over and over, many early blues and rock songs used this form effectively for storytelling. (Of course, the number of verses needed to tell the story determines the number of As used.) Artists such as Bob Dylan and Joni Mitchell popularized the form in the sixties, but it dates back at least as far as many Celtic folklore tunes.

Rehearsal Letters

When it comes time to actually write your lead sheet, the letters used to label the song form should be changed to rehearsal letters. *Rehearsal letters* serve as section cues, marking time in a song and functioning as reference points for rehearsing musicians. They are not repeated like song form letters. A new rehearsal letter should be assigned to each song section that must be written out.

For example, if a lead sheet has an ABABCAB form, and none of the Bs are identical harmonically or in the number of bars, all three B sections must be written out separately and labeled with a different rehearsal letter (so that the musicians know which B section to refer to in rehearsing or performing the song).

Song Form Letters		Rehearsal Letters
A	→	A
B	→	B
A	→	C
B	→	D
C	→	E
A	→	F
B	→	G

Even though these B sections may all sound similar, if a shortcut symbol such as repeat brackets, D.S., or D.C. cannot be used and each section must be written out, then each must logically be given its own rehearsal letter.

As an additional aid to the musicians reading your lead sheet, and to help rehearsals proceed more smoothly, number each or every other measure of your lead sheet or chord chart. (If word cues or symbols are in the way, number just the first measure of every new staff line.) Numbering saves time because it allows musicians to refer to any measure in the music, without having to count measures from a rehearsal letter or other landmark.

The Prechorus

Often in ABAB form, an additional section is added after the A section, following the verse and preceding the chorus. It is usually four to eight bars long and is called the *pre-chorus* or *set-up*. The pre-chorus connects the verse to the chorus, building up musical momentum or adding to the lyric's storyline. In terms of song form, the pre-chorus is generally considered to be a second part of the verse:

A1	Verse
A2	Pre-Chorus
B	Chorus

When labeling the prechorus on a lead sheet, however, give it a new rehearsal letter:

Verse	A
Pre-Chorus	B
Chorus	C

Production and Arrangement Characteristics

Sometimes you'll find production and arrangement characteristics that you want to highlight in your lead sheet. They may not consititute a change in the song's form, but they can be crucial to an effective performance of the song.

Reintro/Outro

When the introduction of a song reappears later in the song, it is called a *reintro* or, if placed at the end of the song, an *outro*. Usually the reintroduction is added to the end of a chorus or the start of a verse and is not considered a separate section, per se.

Breakdown

Sometimes in an arrangement, musical intruments will be removed from a particular song section to give it an empty sound. This is referred to as a *breakdown*. For example, the third time through the chorus of a song, the piano and bass might be taken out while the melody, harmonization, and lyrics remain. Even though the chorus was repeated earlier, the third time through it is written out and given a new rehearsal letter because the musicians have different instructions on how to play.

Interlude

Sometimes a song arrangement will feature an instrumental section, such as a guitar or sax solo, that is played over a verse, chorus, or brand new musical section. Such an *interlude* should be assigned a new rehearsal letter. In fact, it is a good idea to compare the sheet music to the recording to see if the sheet music has included this section, because it is often left out.

Recitation

Recitation is when a singer talks over, or on top of, the music. Write the word "recitation" or "spoken" next to the rehearsal letter assigned to the musical section where the recitation occurs.

Modulation

Changing from one key to another, *modulation*, is usually done at the end of a song. If, for example, the last chorus modulates up a half step, write it out separately from any previous repeats, giving it a new key signature and rehearsal letter.

Introductions

Introductions can pose special problems for the lead sheet writer. Many songs have a distinctive, identifiable introduction that should be included in a lead sheet or chord chart, but sheet music often omits part or all of an introduction. If this happens, you should create your own. This can be done in at least three ways:

   1) By lifting the introduction from the recording;

   2) By creating an introduction from another part of the sheet music (such as the melody and chord progression of the verse or chorus); or

   3) By writing your own original introduction.

Using a *riff* (a main melodic figure) or a chord progression taken from the verse or the chorus can help set the mood of the song. However, in some instances a singer might choose to begin the song out of tempo *(rubato)*, in which case the piano player should simply strike a single chord to help the singer find the starting note.

Endings

Endings are similarly important to a song; they can help create a sense of closure and completion— if an ending is left out of a lead sheet or chord chart, and there are several musicians playing, they may all end on different chords or at different times! There are a number of standard ways to end a song and avoid this confusion:

Tag Endings

In a *tag ending,* the last two to four bars of a song are repeated as a summation of the lyric—a final statement. The title of the song, for instance, might be repeated, reinforcing the song's main idea. Tags often come in a series of three or more. The last repetition of a tag may be sung *a cappella* (without accompaniment). To signal the musicians to stop playing, either draw the "railroad tracks" symbol (//) or write the word "Tacet" where the musicians are to stop.

Ritarding an Ending

To *ritard* an ending is to slacken the tempo gradually. This is indicated by the word "ritard," placed above the measure where the slowing-down process begins. Tag endings and ritard endings are often combined. For example, a songwriter may want the title to be repeated three times at the end of the song and the final repeat to be slowed down for added emphasis. If the singer is to hold out the final note, draw a *fermata* symbol (⌢) over the note or chord to be held.

To end the song abruptly, draw a marcato accent mark (∧) over the final note or write some kind of rhythmic notation.

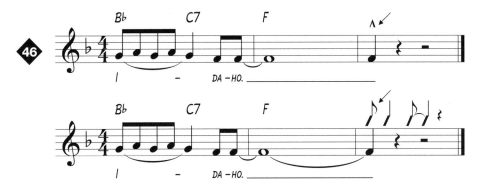

Vamping

One good way to end an up-tempo song is to return to the original riff used in the introduction and vamp on it—to *vamp* simply means to repeat a riff until the singer cues the musicians to stop playing. A vamp can also be based on a repeated chord progression that was introduced at the beginning or played elsewhere during the song.

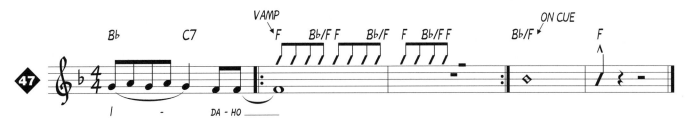

Unexpected Endings

Altered chords, or "surprise" chords, can make effective endings to songs. A listener might expect to hear a I chord, for example, but instead be taken on a brief detour through a ♭VI, ♭VII, ♭II, or iv chord, before finally resolving to the tonic.

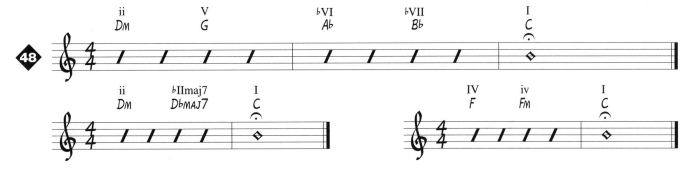

A song might also end with a **deceptive cadence**, where the dominant chord (V7) resolves to a chord other than the tonic (I).

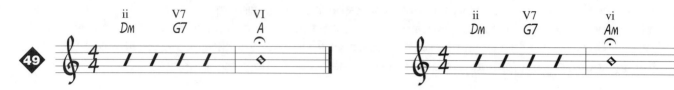

A song in a minor key can end with a **Picardy third**, in which the third degree of the minor tonic (i) is raised to create an unexpected but pleasant-sounding major tonic (I).

Popular Endings

These two endings work well with swing tunes and jazz standards:

The Duke Ellington Ending

The Count Basie Ending

These two are frequently used for rock 'n' roll and R&B:

The Descending Bass Ending

The Ascending Bass Ending

Chapter Six

6 THE ROAD MAP

If you were planning to drive somewhere that you'd never been to before, you would want good directions on how to get there. You would also probably want the most direct route. Musicians want the same thing when following a lead sheet or chord chart. They want easy-to-follow directions that will take them through a song without getting them lost.

Just as some street routes are better than others, some ways of getting through a song are better than others. The main goal for the lead sheet writer is always *to condense, but not confuse!* This is accomplished through the correct use of Road Signs—symbols and terms that tell a musician *where* to go—and Road Condition Indicators—symbols and terms that tell *how* he or she is to get there.

Road Signs

Much like actual road signs, musical Road Signs are directional; they tell a musician to skip ahead, go back, stop, and so on. Road Signs not only help the musician, they also save you time, energy, and space when writing out lead sheets.

Repeat Brackets

Repeat brackets tell the musician to repeat a section of music. (When used at the beginning of a song, the first of the two brackets is omitted.)

Multiple Endings

The first time the musician finishes a section of music within the repeat brackets, he or she uses one ending; the second time through, he or she uses the second ending

Simile Mark

This sign, written within a measure, indicates that a previous measure or group of measures should be repeated.

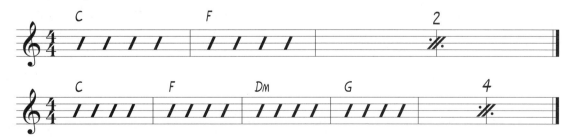

D.C. (Da Capo)

"Da Capo" is an Italian phrase that means "from the head." The letters "*D.C.*," written above or on the staff at the end of a passage, tell the musician to return to the beginning of the song (the "head") and play it again.

D.S. (Dal Segno)

"Dal Segno" is an Italian phrase that means "from the sign." The letters "*D.S.* (𝄋)" written on or above the staff, tell the musician to go back, find the (𝄋) sign, and play from that point forward again.

To Coda (⊕)

These words, written on or above the staff, tell the musician to skip to the coda sign (⊕) near the end of the song and play from there to the end. When writing your lead sheet, it is a good idea to leave a blank staff line before the coda section, to make it easy to spot.

D.C. al Coda (⊕)

Written on or above the staff, these words instruct the musician to return to the beginning and play until the words "*To Coda* ⊕," then skip to the coda sign (⊕) and play to the end of the song.

D.S. 𝄋 al Coda (⊕)

Written on or above the staff, these words tell the musician to return to the (𝄋) sign and play until the words "*To Coda* ⊕," then skip to the coda sign (⊕) and play to the end.

Fine

Written below the staff, "Fine" signals the end of a song.

D.C. al Fine

These words, written on or above the staff, instruct the musician to return to the beginning of the song and play until the "Fine" indication.

D.S. 𝄋 al Fine

These words, written on or above the staff, instruct the musician to return to the (𝄋) sign and play until the word "Fine."

V.S.

These letters, written on the staff line at the end of a section where there is extra space, tell the musician to skip to the next line or page where there is music. "V.S." stands for "volti subito," but it might be easier to think of it as meaning "vacant space." There are three common ways to indicate empty space on a lead sheet or chord chart:

- Write "V.S." on the staff line.

- Draw a squiggly line in the empty space.

- Use liquid paper or relabel type to completely cover the empty measure.

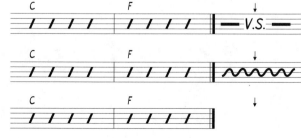

Double Bars

To indicate the end of a phrase or section, place two vertical barlines at the end of the appropriate measure. To indicate the end of an entire song, the second line should be drawn thick.

Multiple Bar Rests

To indicate more than one bar of silence, a number indicating the number of bars of rest is written above the staff. Centered beneath it, filling the second space, is a thick black line. If only some of the instruments rest, indicate clearly which rest and which continue playing.

Rules of the Road

- Write repeat brackets in bold to catch the musician's attention.

- Draw back-to-back repeat brackets separately.

- Never make a musician count back more than four bars. If more than four bars are to be repeated, use repeat brackets instead of a simile (✗) sign.

- Try to keep simile (✗) signs on the same staff as the measures to repeated, so that the musician doesn't have to look back at a previous staff line.

- Do not use repeat brackets within repeat brackets—using more than one set of repeat brackets within the same section is confusing. To repeat smaller sections of music within a larger section, use simile (✗) signs, or write out the smaller section of music.

- When repeating a section more than once, or when using multiple endings within repeat brackets, tell the musician how many times the section is to be played, not how many times it is "repeated." "Play 3 times" tells the musician to play the section a total of three times. ("Play 3x" is also an acceptable indication.)

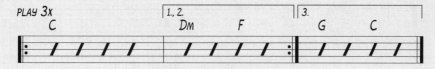

Just as real road signs are designed to catch a driver's attention with bright colors, reflectors, or lights, musical Road Signs should catch the musician's eye. I like to highlight all of the signs with a highlighter. I also draw boxes around the D.C., D.S., Coda, and Fine signs. Then from the boxed sign, I draw a small arrow pointing to the end of the staff where the sign occurs.

I think this additional step is important, because some musicians look for indicators below the staff line, even though the usual practice is to write the sign on or above the staff. It's also particularly helpful in reading a lead sheet that is busy with many melody notes, several verses of lyrics, and numerous chord changes.

Road Condition Indicators

Much like actual road condition signs that direct a driver to slow down, proceed with caution, etc., musical Road Condition Indicators are descriptive; they tell a musician to play faster, slower, softer, louder, etc.

Dynamics

Dynamics are fluctuations in intensity or loudness. They make a song more interesting. Dynamic indications should be placed beneath the staff, either directly below or slightly before the note or section affected.

pp (pianissimo)	very soft
p (piano)	soft
mp (mezzo piano)	moderately soft
f (mezzo forte)	moderately loud
mf (forte)	loud
ff (fortissimo)	very loud

crescendo – Increase volume gradually. The abbreviation "cresc." or a wedge-shaped symbol pointing to the left is written below the staff.

decrescendo – Decrease volume gradually. The abbreviations "decresc." or "dimin." or a wedge-shaped symbol pointing to the right is written below the staff.

Tempo

Tempo markings are written at the start of a section or at the beginning of the section affected. In writing lead sheets, it is perfectly acceptable to use English words like "slow," "fast," "moderate," etc. The Italian terms below are included for your own reference. The second set of terms below are used to indicate changes of tempo. You would be wise to learn and use them in your lead sheets.

largo	large, broad, slow
adagio	slow, leisurely
andante	moderately slow, walking
moderato	moderate
allegro	lively, brisk, cheerful
presto	fast, rapid

ritard – slow down.

rubato – suspend tempo; singer sets or changes pace at will, while musicians follow singer's lead. This term is usually written at the beginning of the affected section, next to the rehearsal letter.

fermata (⌒) – hold a note indefinitely until cued to stop or to play on.

accelerando – speed up; increase tempo.

a tempo – begin or resume at tempo; usually written after a fermata, //, tacet, ritard, or rubato indication.

l'istesso tempo – return to original tempo; usually written at the start of a section, after a section in which the tempo or time signature has changed. For example, if the A section is ♩=75, and the B section is ♩=120, the next A section would be marked "l'istesso tempo," signaling a return to the original tempo of ♩=75.

Articulations

Articulations further explain how a note should be sounded. They are generally placed directly above or below the notehead affected.

staccato – detached, separated; play in a somewhat abrubt and choppy manner, shortening the value of the note. When a staccato mark (·) is placed over a quarter note, for example, the note's duration is decreased by half a beat.

tenuto – held; sustain the note for its full value.

accent – stress the note over other notes and play it for its full value; it should be played harder than a nearby note without an accent mark.

marcato – play note distinctly and with emphasis; similar to an accent mark, except that the note is not played for its full value—it is slightly detached.

slur – a curved line drawn over two or more notes; signals a musician to play the group of notes in a legato fashion.

slide – tells a guitar or bass player to slide into a desired note.

grace note – a note added as an embellishment before the main note. Smaller than a regular-size note, a grace note is written as a small eighth note with a tiny slanted line drawn through the stem, which always goes up. The grace note is placed directly in front of the main note and is connected by a slur.

trill – two or more consecutive tones played in quick alternation.

tremolo – the rapid trembling or repetition of a note. When playing a guitar or other string instrument, it is the fast repetition of one note; when singing, it is the slight, continuous fluctuation of pitch around one note; when playing a piano, it is the rapid alternation of two or more notes.

glissando – instructs the piano player to drag his or her finger up or down the keys before playing the downbeat or main chord. Usually abbreviated as "gliss" and indicated by a wavy line leading from one note to another.

choke or **mute** – to deaden or muffle a sound; often used by a guitar player when arpeggiating or playing an eighth-note rhythmic pattern.

legato – the opposite of staccato; tells a musician to play smoothly, connectedly, without pause.

Other Indicators

poco a poco – means "little by little." This term can be used with any of the dynamics or tempo indications described above. For example, "dimin. poco a poco" written beneath the staff tells a musician to decrease in volume little by little.

col (a.k.a., cogli, coll', colla, colle, or collo) – Italian for "with the." This is another multipurpose term, often used when two instruments are to play the same part. For instance, "piano col bass" means that the piano reads the bass part and plays along with the bass. "Colla voce" is a common instruction that indicates the instruments should follow the vocal melody.

sans – means "without." This term is used when an instrument or voice is removed from a song section. For example, "sans guitar," placed above the staff at the start of a chorus, would tell the guitar player not to play during that chorus. (This could also be written as "gtr. tacet.")

simile – tells a musician to continue playing a particular rhythm or part similar to the way in which it was played in the measures just previous. For example, a guitar pattern written in rhythmic notation for several measures could be followed by the word "simile."

8va/8vb – tells a musician to play one octave higher or lower.

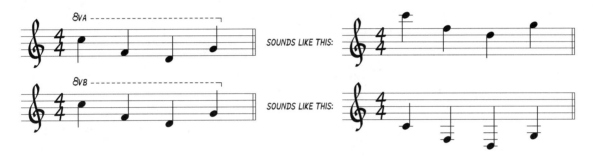

loco – cancels a previous indication (most often "8va" or "8vb") and signals a return to a normal playing position.

tacet – means "silent"; signals a musican to stop playing.

railroad tracks (//) – stop playing abruptly, and resume when cued.

tutti – Found most often in orchestral pieces, "tutti" indicates that all performers play at once, usually the same part.

unison – This word usually indicates two voices singing the same melody line after singing in harmony, or two instruments playing together after playing separate parts. The parts are identical but may be in different octaves.

divisi – The opposite of unison, "divisi" signals the voices to sing in harmony and the instruments to play separately.

sotto voce – instructs a singer to sing in a very soft voice, almost a whisper.

Chapter Seven
TRANSPOSITION

As a lead sheet writer, I am often asked to transpose a song, usually into a lower key. Frequently, singers sing in one key for a recording but sing in another key for a live performance. They might sing low notes better in the morning and high notes better in the evening…The reasons for transposing go on and on. And it's not just singers—transposition can also make life easier for the rhythm section or for an instrumental soloist. Some types of music just sound better in certain keys. Rock songs, for example, sound good in the key of E because a guitarist can make use of the open strings on his or her instrument.

Transposition can be tricky business, though, particularly for the beginner. This chapter shows you, step by step, how to transpose a melody or a chord progression, as well as how to recognize and deal with altered chords, borrowed chords, and modulations. We'll assume that you already have a lead sheet, a chord chart, or some sheet music—in other words, that you have a melody and chord progression to work with—and that you are ready to transpose.

Transposing a Melody

Step 1: Identify the key

Identifying the key of a song can be as easy as looking at the sheet music for a key signature. If you don't have sheet music, the situation is just a little trickier. Basically, you've got two options:

(1) Find the tonic note

The tonic is the 1st degree, or root, of the scale on which your melody is based. It should be the note that seems the most at rest, the most stable, to your ear. Experiment with your tune. Try singing or playing it slowly and stopping mid-phrase. Does it sound resolved or completed to you? Probably not. The tonic is often the first or last note of a melody or a phrase, but not always.

(2) Count your sharps and flats

Assuming you have the melody written out, try to assemble a scale from its pitches, paying particular attention to any sharped or flatted notes. Compare this collection of notes to any of the twelve scales of the Transposition Chart. You should be able to find a match.

If you have a key signature, but you're still stuck identifying the key, refer to the Circle of Fifths chart in Chapter 2. Keep in mind that a single key signature can refer to both a major key and its relative minor, so you need to determine which key—major or minor—is intended.

This will be our sample tune. Try to determine its key:

Transposition Chart

Chord Numerals

	I	ii	iii	IV	V	vi	vii°
	C	Dm	Em	F	G	Am	B°
	F	Gm	Am	B♭	C	Dm	E°
	B♭	Cm	Dm	E♭	F	Gm	A°
	E♭	Fm	Gm	A♭	B♭	Cm	D°
	A♭	B♭m	Cm	D♭	E♭	Fm	G°
	D♭	E♭m	Fm	G♭	A♭	B♭m	C°
	C♯	D♯m	E♯m	F♯	G♯	A♯m	B♯°
Major Keys	G♭	A♭m	B♭m	C♭	D♭	E♭m	F°
	F♯	G♯m	A♯m	B	C♯	D♯m	E♯°
	B	C♯m	D♯m	E	F♯	G♯m	A♯°
	E	F♯m	G♯m	A	B	C♯m	D♯°
	A	Bm	C♯m	D	E	F♯m	G♯°
	D	Em	F♯m	G	A	Bm	C♯°
	G	Am	Bm	C	D	Em	F♯°
	1	2	3	4	5	6	7

Scale Degrees

Step 2: Write out the scale

Once you've identified the key, write out its scale. Look at the bottom row of the Transposition Chart for the scale degree numbers that correspond to the notes of your scale, and place those numbers below the scale.

Our example is in the key of D major, so we'll write out a D major scale:

Step 3: Assign a scale degree number to each melody note

First identify each note of your melody by its pitch name. Then, using your numbered scale from Step 2 as a reference, place the appropriate scale degree below.

Notice that in our example only four different pitches are used:

D	F♯	A	C♯
1	3	5	7

45

Step 4: Choose a new key, and write out its scale

Presumably you've already chosen a new key by the time you're ready to transpose. Your decision will likely have been based on considerations like melodic range, ease of fingering, ease of sightreading, better tone production, etc.

Write out the scale of the key into which you are transposing, and number each note as you did with the first scale. We will transpose our example to B♭ major:

Step 5: Transpose the melody into its new key

Take the numbers you assigned to your melody in its original key (Step 3) and match them with the scale degree numbers of your new scale (Step 4) to find the corresponding melody notes in the new key. Basically, the process should look like this:

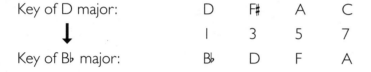

Once you've determined the corresponding notes in your new key, just plug these new notes into the numbers of your "old" melody—in this case, every D note in the old melody becomes a B♭ in the new one, every F♯ becomes a D, every A becomes an F, and so on.

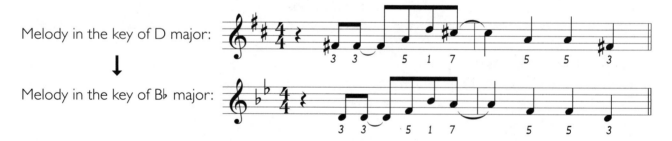

A Note about Accidentals

When transposing accidentals, a raised half step is labeled with a plus sign (+), and a lowered half step is labeled with a minus sign (-). The 5th degree of a scale, for example, is +5 when raised and -5 when lowered. This example is from a C major scale.

The actual accidental may differ when a melody is transposed—a sharp may become a natural, a natural may become a flat, etc.—but the scale degree must be raised or lowered by the exact same interval.

Transposing a Chord Progression

The steps to transposing a chord progression are virtually identical to those for transposing a melody; however, instead of referring to the arabic numbers at the bottom of the Transposition Chart, you will refer to the Roman numerals at the top.

Step 1: Identify the key

Once again, identifying the key is a matter of either looking at the key signature, finding the tonic (I) chord, or comparing the chords in your progression with chords in the keys of the Transposition Chart. This is our sample progression:

D   G   F#m   Bm

Step 2: Write out all chords in the key

Once you've identified the key, write out the chords based on its scale. Look at the top row of the Transposition Chart for the Roman numerals that correspond to each chord, and write those numerals below the chords. Our example is again in the key of D major:

D	Em	F#m	G	A	Bm	C#°
I	ii	iii	IV	V	vi	vii°

Step 3: Number each chord in your progression

Using the numbered chords from Step 2 as a reference, apply the appropriate Roman numeral to each chord in your progression. Notice that, out of a possible seven chords, our progression uses just four:

D	G	F#m	Bm
I	IV	iii	vi

Step 4: Choose a new key and write out its chords

Write out the chords of the key into which you are transposing, and label them with Roman numerals as you did with the first key.

Our new key will be B♭ major:

B♭	Cm	Dm	E♭	F	Gm	A°
I	ii	iii	IV	V	vi	vii°

Step 5: Transpose your chords to the new key

Take the Roman numerals assigned to your chord progression in its original key (Step 3) and match them with the corresponding Roman numerals of your new key (Step 4) to find the chords in your new key. The process looks roughly like this:

Key of D major:	D	G	F#m	Bm
↓	I	IV	iii	vi
Key of B♭ major:	B♭	E♭	Dm	Gm

The number system for transposing chords helps you learn how chord progressions function and makes the job of changing keys simple and fast.

Two Important Transposition Rules

When transposing from one key to another, keep in mind the following two rules.

Rule 1: The quality of chords always stays the same

Observe this example, in which a chord progression is transposed from C to F:

Key of C major:	C	G+	Am	Fmaj7	Dm7♭5	G7
↓	I	V+	vi	IVmaj7	iim7♭5	V7
Key of F major:	F	C+	Dm	B♭maj7	Gm7♭5	C7

Only the letter names change; the qualities of the individual chords (major, minor, augmented, etc.) do not.

Rule 2: Flats and sharps don't mix

This rule applies to songs that stick to a particular key—not necessarily to accidentals that may occur from time to time within a piece. As an example, consider the following chord progression in the key of C. If we decided to transpose it up by a half step, the chord chart could be written out in either of two keys: D-flat or C-sharp.

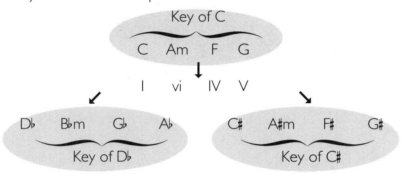

But a hodge-podge of both keys would be incorrect, as in these examples:

Choice of enharmonic spelling—the two different letter names for the same note or chord—must be consistent within a key. This same rule also applies to melody lines. This melody in the key of C could be transposed either of two ways:

But the following transpositions would be incorrect:

In fact, if you transpose using the step-by-step method outlined in this chapter and refer to the Transposition Chart, you shouldn't run into problems with this. The problem is more likely to occur when *transcribing* a melody or progression—particularly in an unfamiliar key. (So consider yourself warned!)

Altered Chords

All of the chords listed horizontally on the Transposition Chart are diatonic to the keys that they follow. This means that the notes that make up the chords can be found in the key or scale to which they are referenced. An Em chord, for instance, is diatonic to the key of C major because it consists only of the notes E, G, and B, all of which can be found in a C major scale. It is a iii chord in that key because it is a minor chord based on the 3rd degree of the scale.

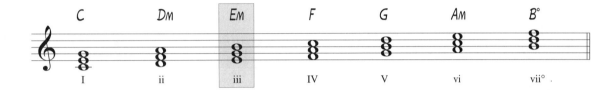

A chord can be altered if one or more of its notes are raised or lowered a half step from the diatonic key. Lowering the E and B of an Em chord, for instance, results in an E♭ chord. The E♭ chord is no longer diatonic to the key of C—the notes E♭ and B♭ do not belong to the C major scale—but it can still be analyzed in the key of C if we consider it an altered chord and relabel it appropriately. In this case, it would be a ♭III chord because it is a major chord based on the flatted 3rd scale degree.

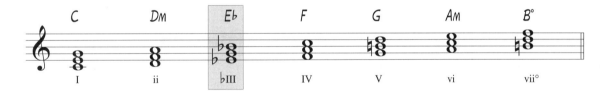

When transposing altered chords, keep in mind that naturals may become flats, and sharps may become naturals. For example, a ♭III chord in the key of C major is E♭, but a ♭III in the key of A major is C. Both, however, are still labeled ♭III in a Roman numeral analysis.

Parallel Keys and Borrowed Chords

Often, altered chords work well within a diatonic major key because they belong to the key's *parallel minor*. A parallel minor is a minor key built on the same first note as a major key of the same name. For instance, the parallel minor of C major is C minor; the parallel minor of G major is G minor; and so on.

Unlike relative major and minor keys, which share all the same notes of a scale, parallel major and minor do *not* share the same scale. They do share the same starting note, however, and typically the 4th and 5th scale degrees as well. Because their scales are very different, though, the chords diatonic to these scales are also very different.

Below is a comparison of the chords of C major and C natural minor. Notice that not a single chord from one scale can be found in the other:

C Major:	C	Dm	Em	F	G	Am	B
C Minor:	Cm	D	Eb	Fm	Gm	Ab	Bb

If a song in a major key borrows chords from the parallel minor, those chords are considered chromatic to the major key and are labeled as altered chords. Below is an example of a chord progression in C major that uses chords borrowed from C minor:

The Eb and Bb are **borrowed chords** from C minor and are considered "altered" in the major key. Similarly, if a song in a minor key borrows chords from the parallel major, they should also be considered "altered." The chords Em and G in the melody below are borrowed from C major, making them altered chords in the key of C minor.

Secondary Dominants and Modulation

In a diatonic major key, there is only one dominant chord, the V7. The V7 is a powerful chord. It is one of the most dissonant chords in a major key, and it has the strongest pull to resolve to the tonic I chord. Sometimes, however, additional dominant chords do appear in a progression. These chords (which contain accidentals and are therefore yet another type of altered chord) typically function as dominant chords to other chords in the progression and are referred to as "secondary dominants."

A **secondary dominant** is any chord that functions as a dominant to a chord other than the tonic, or I chord. Because of its unusual function, a secondary dominant chord can be labeled two different ways. Consider this example in the key of C major:

The E7 chord is an altered chord because its 3rd degree, G#, is chromatic to the key of C. But it is also a secondary dominant chord—a diatonic V7 chord in the key of A major. For transposition purposes, however, it is easier to label the E7 as an altered chord (III7) than as a true secondary dominant (V/vi), so the altered labeling is preferable in this case.

Because the dominant is such a powerful chord, the sound of a secondary dominant chord may lead the listener to think that the song is **modulating**, or changing keys. If the secondary dominant is followed by a string of chords outside the original key, then a modulation probably has in fact occurred, and this should be acknowledged in your analysis:

Secondary dominants are one means by which a songwriter or arranger can modulate from one key to another. Two other common means are by pivot chord and by direct modulation. A *pivot chord* is a transitional chord that is common to two keys but functions differently in each key. Pivot chords can be used alone—when modulating to the relative major or minor, for instance—or in conjuction with secondary dominant chords. In the latter case, the pivot chord is the last chord to be analyzed in the original key:

In *direct modulation*, no transition is offered between the two keys. Because there is no pivot chord or secondary dominant to smooth the transition and prepare the listener, the key change feels very abrupt. Often, songwriters use direct modulation to grab the listener's attention or to create a dramatic effect.

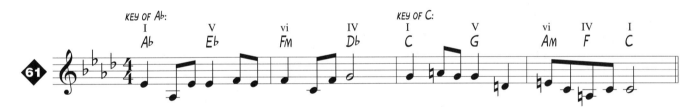

Some Tips on Secondary Dominants

← Keep in mind that secondary dominants may not always resolve to the expected diatonic chord. In this example, E7 is expected to resolve to Am— because E7 is the V7 chord of A minor—but instead it resolves unexpectedly to F.

Also, though seldom used in pop songs, the vii° chord can substitute for a dominant V7 chord in a progression, or for a secondary dominant. This → is because the vii° and the V7 share three common tones.

Chapter Eight

8 TO SLASH OR NOT TO SLASH?

Notating a melody is fairly straightforward work—difficult at times, but straightforward. Notating an accompaniment, however, is another story. You have a lot of options when you create a chord chart for an accompaniment. The simplest method to use is **slash notation**, which tells an accompanist what chords to play and how many beats each chord should receive:

The above slashes tell a musician to play four beats of a C chord, two beats of an F chord, and then two beats of a G chord. Notice that the slashes do *not* indicate what style the chords should be played in, what voicings should be used, or what rhythmic feel the accompaniment might have—this is all up to an individual musician's interpretation. Slashes only require that a musician keep time with the song and change chords on the appropriate beats.

In most cases, a single-staff slash chord chart will be all that you'll need; however, from time to time, you may want to get more detailed. Your chord chart can be as simple or as complex as you like, depending on the the type of notation you use and the instrumentation you require.

Condensing Sheet Music

Typically, sheet music is presented in systems of either three staves or two. In a *three-staff system*, the top staff shows the vocal melody while the bottom two staves show the instrumental accompaniment. In a *two-staff system*, the vocal melody is combined with the upper part of the accompaniment.

In both cases, the arrangement of the music typically restricts the accompanist to playing the exact same melody as the singer, along with a bass line and some additional harmonies. Such sheet music can be readily condensed into a *single-staff* slash chord chart, for several reasons:

- Most singers *don't want* the accompanist doubling their melody. In performance, they may decide they want to change a note here or there, or they may just make a mistake—which really sticks out if the accompanist is hitting the "right" notes.

- Exact chord voicings, written out on the first or second staff, are usually unnecessary because both pianists and guitarists can typically read the chord symbols written above the staff and supply their own chord voicings.

- Written bass parts can often be replaced with a simple direction or accompanimental term, which tells the piano or bass player to follow the chord symbols and improvise an appropriate note or pattern for every chord.

If a short description will not give the piano or bass player enough information to play a part convincingly, then the part should be written out, and the chord chart should include a second or third staff. A single chord chart may incorporate single, double, and even triple staff systems:

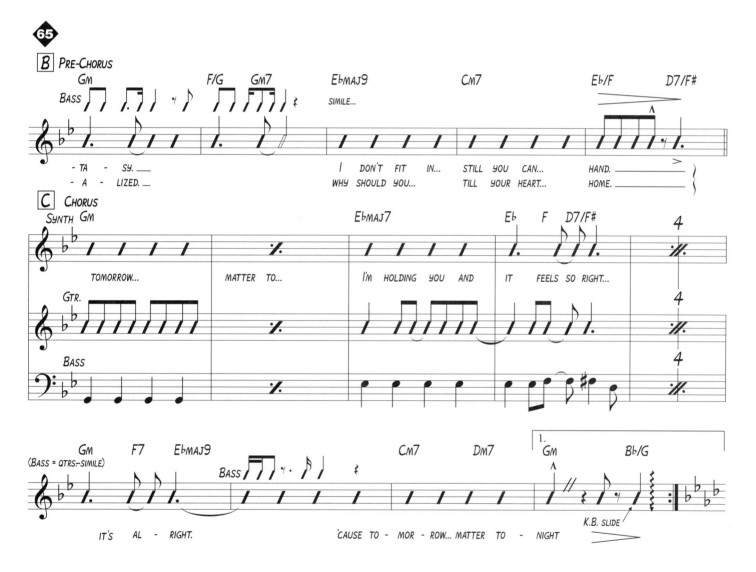

Switching back and forth, however, can confuse a musician—so do this only when absolutely necessary, and indicate clearly which parts are played by which instruments. Also, draw a bracket to the left of double or triple staff lines.

Sometimes, sheet music shows the vocal melody holding or resting, while in the second staff, the instrumental accompaniment stops imitating the vocal melody and plays independently. If this instrumental part is important to the song, it should be notated in the chord chart. In the example below, the melody is held out in the first staff, while a *fill*—a brief instrumental melody line—is written out in the second staff.

When making a chord chart from sheet music, use slashes if the accompaniment is imitating the vocal melody, but transfer important accompanimental fills (piano or guitar riffs) when the vocal melody is holding or resting.

Rhythmic Notation and Top-Note Voicing

Unlike slashes, which allow a musician to play whatever part he or she wants to within a song's musical style, *rhythmic notation* limits a musician to playing a specific rhythm. Rhythmic notation is useful for songs in which chords change on beats other than the downbeat, or in cases when a specific rhythmic pattern is crucial to a song's identity.

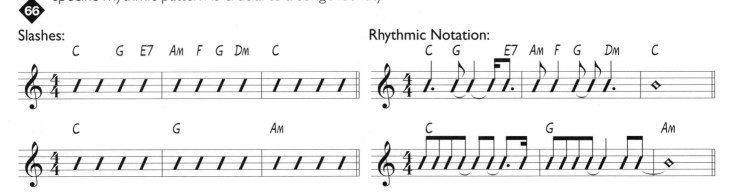

This system of using symbols to represent durations of notes and their relationship to each other in time is used in place of musical notes and shows only rhythm, not pitch:

Even more specific than rhythmic notation, *top-note voicing* tells a musician what rhythms to play *and* the top note of each chord voicing. For example, this excerpt from the introduction of "Tomorrow Doesn't Matter Tonight" is notated in top-note voicing. Notice that the stem of each note extends below the notehead; this signals the musician to play an entire chord beneath the top note.

54

Top-note voicing can be used to help identify a signature part of a song—such as the top notes of a guitar riff—or to help a singer find the right melody notes.

Slashes, rhythmic notation, and top-note voicing can also be combined in one chord chart:

As a beginning chord chart writer, you may have difficulty recognizing important instrumental parts; you may be uncertain when to write slashes and when to use more specific notation. If in doubt, *stick with slashes.* Even though the instrumental parts make the song more recognizable, they are not essential for accompaniment, and the song will still work with just the proper chords.

Accompanimental Terms

When paired with an appropriate *style description* such as "Rock," "Country Two-Step," or "Ballad" (placed at the beginning of a lead sheet or chord chart) the following terms can substitute for writing out a particular piano, guitar, or bass accompaniment in full.

- **ostinato** – a repeated musical pattern, which often serves as a musical hook in the introduction or vamp.

- **arpeggio** – notes of a chord played in succession, one note at a time.

- **broken chord** – similar to an arpeggio except that, of the three or more notes of a chord, at least two are played at the same time, followed by the rest of the chord, usually in a repeating rhythmic pattern.

- **broken octave** – two notes, an octave apart, played in succession.

• **bass = qtrs** – tells a bassist to play quarter notes in the bass part. This type of abbreviation can be applied to any instrument as long as the rhythm is constant (e.g., "pno. = whole notes" or "gtr. = 8th notes"), and the choice of notes is fairly obvious.

Instrument Ranges

Each instrument in the rhythm section has both a written musical range and a sounding musical range. For the piano, these two ranges are identical, but for the guitar and bass, the written range is one octave higher than the actual sounding range—so that the notes fall on the staff and not below it. You should be aware of these ranges if you're notating a part specifically for these instruments.

Piano

The written and sounding ranges for the piano are:

Chords played with the right hand (RH) generally sound good in the middle and upper ranges—middle C and up. The left hand (LH) typically plays lower chord voicings and bass lines. Be careful with the lower range, because if chords are voiced too low on the piano, they sound "muddy." Also be aware that, even though the piano has a wide range, many musicians use keyboards and synthesizers that have fewer octaves.

If you want to indicate that a part in the left hand is to be played higher—in the treble clef range—change the bass clef to a treble clef for as long as the part lasts. When the part ends, return to the bass clef; this will signal the musician to return to playing in the lower register. This rule also applies to right hand parts that are to be played lower, in the bass clef.

Also, when writing piano parts for both clefs, be sure to align the parts correctly so that they are easy to read.

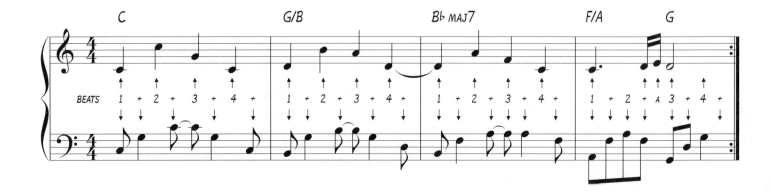

Guitar

Guitar is notated using the treble clef. Its written range is from a low E to a high B:

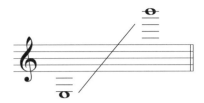

Many guitars can go a note or two higher than the above range, and all guitars can be be detuned to reach several notes lower, but this is a good standard range to follow. Keep in mind that the guitar's sounding range is actually one octave lower.

Bass

Bass guitar is notated in the bass clef. Its written range is from a very low E to a high C:

Like the guitar, the bass sounds one octave lower than it is written.

Drums

It's generally not necessary to write out entire drum parts; a good style description will usually suffice. However, writing a specific drum part at the start of a chart, or a new section where the drum feel changes, can be helpful. In such cases, write one, two, or even four bars of drum indications below a single staff, followed by the word "simile."

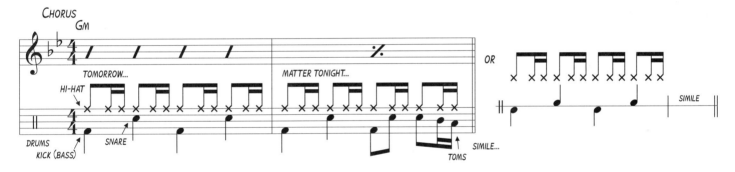

Instrument Abbreviations

Because the amount of space on a chord chart or lead sheet is limited, the names of instruments are often abbreviated. Below are some of the most common abbreviations. Many writers capitalize all letters in an abbreviation, others don't. Also, some include the period while others don't.

Piano	pno.	Tom tom	tom.
Synthesizer	synth.	High hat	hi hat/h.h.
Guitar	gtr.	Cymbal	cym.
Acoustic guitar	acous. gtr.	Tambourine	tamb.
Electric guitar	elec. gtr.	Saxophone	sax.
Bass	bs.	Trumpet	trpt.
Drums	drm.	Trombone	trb.
Snare drum	sn./s.d.	Strings	stg.
Bass drum	b.d.		

Chapter Nine

SHEET MUSIC → CHORD CHART

Remember Brandi's audition? She learned the hard way that traditional sheet music isn't necessarily the best way to present a song. Too many pages, no clear tempo indication… Her music didn't even seem to be in the right key! Unfortunately, most sheet music is geared toward the amateur home player, not to the professional musician. Rest assured, however; creating a lead sheet or chord chart for a song is really fairly easy if you already have the sheet music for it. After all, you've got the melody, the harmony, the rhythms, and the lyrics all right there in front of you—over half your work is done. You just have to translate, or *transcribe*, the song into another medium.

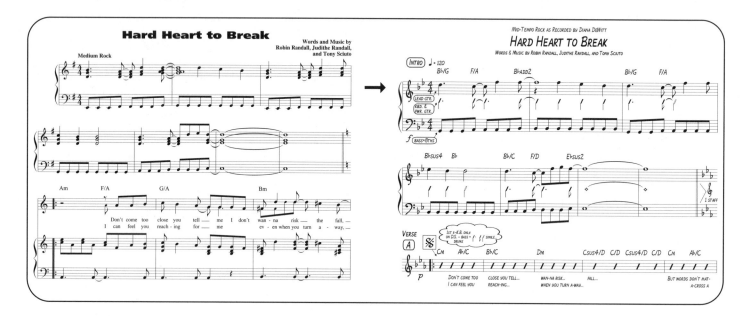

This chapter shows you, step by step, how to create a chord chart for a song based on its sheet music. As an example, we'll create one for Brandi's audition song, "Hard Heart to Break." In our example, we'll refer to both sheet music *and* a recording, because Brandi wants to model her chord chart after a particular recording that she likes. I suggest that, for the first few songs you try on your own, you do the same—it generally makes the process more meaningful and enjoyable. Our goal here will be to rely on the sheet music for the nuts and bolts of the music but to look to the recording for things like arrangement, key, tempo, style, etc.

Step 1: The recording

If you're modeling your chord chart after a particular recording, this first step is crucial. Usually, recordings and sheet music differ in their arrangement. The basic elements of the song, such as the form and melody, remain the same, but how the sections are presented may change. Often, sheet music is condensed; it may leave out instrumental sections or ignore repeated choruses and verses found in a recording. Or just the opposite might be true; sheet music may be pages longer than it needs to be because shortcut terms and symbols such as repeat brackets and D.S. signs have not been used.

Your first step, then, is to listen to the recording while following along with the sheet music. Make notes in the margins, in pencil, of how and where the two differ, if at all. Don't worry about individual notes or rhythms, just look at the overall form. If there's a section written out that you think could be condensed with a repeat sign, make a note of it. If there's a catchy intro riff in the recording you want to make sure to include in your chord chart, make a note of that. If you don't have a recording to compare to your sheet music, then take the time to read through the sheet music mentally, making a note of things like style, key signature, sections, and so on. Try to identify each section as a verse, chorus, bridge, solo, etc.

Here's the sheet music for "Hard Heart to Break." Follow along with it while listening to the audio, and note any differences you find. Label each section appropriately (e.g. intro, verse, chorus, etc.).

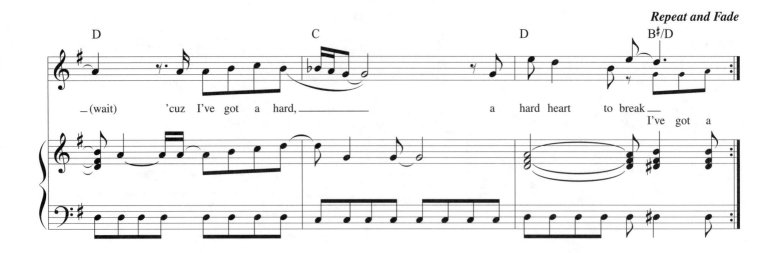

While listening to "Hard Heart to Break," Brandi notices that the chorus repeats the last time through using two different endings. This is *not* indicated in the sheet music, so she writes a brief comment in the margin. Also, the recording's introduction has a distinctive, "signature" guitar riff that she wants to include in her chord chart, so she writes herself a reminder next to the introduction. Brandi then notices that the chord symbols are left out of the introduction. She writes "chords left out of intro" and checks the reintro—there she finds the chord symbols that she'll need to insert.

Step 2: The Form Analysis Chart

Once you're familiar with the sheet music, you're ready to begin breaking down your song using a Form Analysis Chart.

The Form Analysis Chart is the single most useful tool you'll have for laying out a lead sheet or chord chart. It begins with basic information that you'll include at the top of your chord chart—title, artist, key, time signature, and tempo—as well as information that will help you arrange or transpose your song material—like melodic range and style description. The meat of the chart, though, is the grid that asks you to break down the song into sections, label each with a rehearsal letter, count the number measures in it, and add any Road Map instructions or comments. This section gets you to consider how the reader will navigate his or her way through your lead sheet or chord chart.

There is a blank Form Analysis Chart in the appendix. I suggest you make photocopies of it because you will want to use it again and again. Try filling one out for "Hard Heart to Break." Refer to the sheet music and audio, along with your handwritten notes, to help you complete ithe chart. As you go through the song, ask yourself questions like, "Do some sections repeat? Can they be condensed with repeat signs or simile marks? Is there an instrumental solo that should be included?" If you get stuck, just follow Brandi's example:

> After writing the title of the song, Brandi notes the key signature and the time signature. She then writes a style description ("pop/rock"), an indication of who recorded the song

("Aina"), and the authors' names. Brandi notices that the sheet music does not have a metronome marking; it only says "medium rock." To find out the exact tempo, she plays the recording and turns on her metronome, adjusting it to match the tempo of the song. She then proceeds to break down the song, section by section.

Form Analysis Chart

Song Title: ___HARD HEART TO BREAK___

Songwriter/Artist: ___ROBIN RANDALL, JUDITHE RANDALL, TONY SCIUTO, AINA___

Key	Time Signature	Tempo	Melodic Range	Style Description
G	4/4	♩ =120	LOW F# HIGH E ON STAFF	POP/ROCK

Form of Song			Road Map Instructions	Comments
Song Section	Rehearsal Letters	Number of Bars		
INTRO	—	7	THE SAME/WRITE OUT	INCL. GTR.
VS 1	A	8 ⎫	CAN CONDENSE THIS BY	RIFF/NO CHORDS
VS 2	A	8 ⎬	USING REPEAT BRACKETS	MARKED-END DIFF.
PRE-CH	B	8	WRITE OUT	
CH	C	8	" "	
RE-INTRO	—	4	USE AS 1ST ENDING	INCL. GTR. RIFF
			INCL. GTR. RIFF	
VS 3	A	8 ⎫	USE D.S. (%) TO RETURN	
VS 4	A	8 ⎬	TO THIS SECTION/REPEAT GOOD	
PRE-CH	B	8	CONTINUE	
CH	C	8	(SAME AS ABOVE)	
BR	D	9	START OF 2ND ENDING	KEY CHANGE G TO E
CH	E	8	INSTR./GTR. SOLO	
			WRITE OUT/CAN'T D.S. AGAIN	
CH	F	8 ⎫	½ OF CH. BREAKDOWN	FORM DIFFERS
CH	G	8 ⎬	BAR 5 OF CH. – BAND IN	↓
(VAMP)			USE REPEAT BRACKETS	FIGURE OUT
			CH. ENDS DIFF.	ENDINGS
			VAMP w/2 DIFF. ENDINGS	

Additional Notes: SONG NEEDS RHYTHMIC NOTATION IN CERTAIN SECTIONS; CAN USE BASS SIMILE (GIVE RHY. PATTERN); FIGURE OUT CHORDS IN INTRO; SONG CHANGES KEY FROM INTRO (G) TO VERSE (C); FROM PRE-CH (C) TO CHORUS (G) BRIDGE IS IN (E) BACK TO (G) FOR END CHORUS +VAMP

Once you know which sections repeat, which don't, and in what order they follow, you can condense this information even further into a musical Road Map. This will serve as an easy-to-follow guide to creating your chord chart.

Brandi's Road Map

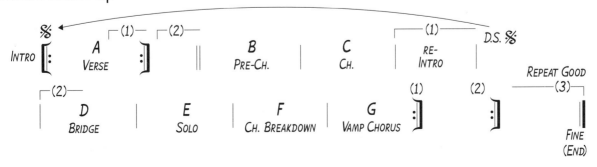

Step 3: The key

Next, you need to consider the key of your song. If you have both sheet music and a recording, compare the two to see if their keys are identical. To do this, play or sing the first few notes of the sheet music's melody, and see if they match the first few notes of the melody on the recording.

Brandi uses her keyboard to play the first note of the vocal melody as it appears on the sheet music. It is an A note on the first word of the lyric *"Don't* come too close..."

Although the sheet music for "Hard Heart to Break" begins with an instrumental introduction in G, when the vocal melody comes in, the key changes to C. So Brandi looks at her Transposition Chart to find the key of C and where the A note would fit into that key. She sees that A is the 6th note of the scale.

	I	ii	iii	IV	V	vi	vii°
Key of C major:	C	Dm	Em	F	G	Am	B°

If the first vocal melody note in the recording is also an A, the keys are the same. Brandi listens to the first melody note of the recording, sings the pitch out loud, and finds it on her keyboard—it is an A! Since the first melody note in both the sheet music and the recording is A, both are in the key of C.

If the melodies do not match, then you need to determine the first note on the recording and use your Transposition Chart to help figure out its key. For example, let's say the recording of "Hard Heart to Break" had a D as the first note of its vocal melody. You already know that this first note is the 6th scale degree of its key, so you look for the key that has D as its 6th scale degree—which is F major—and this would be the key of the recording.

	I	ii	iii	IV	V	vi	vii°
Key of F major:	F	Gm	Am	B♭	C	Dm	E°

Next, consider what key you would prefer the song to be in. Is the current melodic range appropriate for your lead singer or instrumentalist? Is this the best-sounding key for the instruments that will be accompanying you? Is it the easiest key? Will there be ample practice time to get this song down, or will the musicians be sightreading your chart?

Brandi wants to make sure that the melody is well within her vocal range. She studies the sheet music to find the lowest and highest notes. The lowest is an F♯ on the bottom space of the treble clef staff. She circles it. The highest is an E on the top space of the staff.

Brandi knows she hits a powerful E on the staff in her high range, but she's not sure how strong her low F# sounds. She thinks she'd be safer with a range about 2 1/2 steps up. This means she'll have to transpose the song into a higher key.

Even though "Hard Heart to Break" changes from the key of G to the key of C when the vocal melody enters, the song's primary key is G. First, she looks to see what scale degree the E is:

	I	ii	iii	IV	V	vi	vii°
Key of G major:	G	Am	Bm	C	D	Em	F#°

E is the 6th degree of a G major scale. Brandi decides the highest note of the melody should be a G, so she looks for the key on the Transposition Chart that has G as its 6th degree. She sees that the key of B-flat has G as its 6th degree.

	I	ii	iii	IV	V	vi	vii°
Key of B♭ major:	B♭	Cm	Dm	E♭	F	Gm	A°

Therefore, B-flat is the best key for her to perform the song in.

Finally, you're ready to transpose (or *not* to transpose, as the case may be). If you're writing a lead sheet, you'll need to transpose both melody and chords; if you're writing a chord chart, just the chords.

Looking more closely at her sheet music, Brandi notices that "Hard Heart to Break" actually passes through three different keys.

She's already decided that the song's primary key is G major and that she wants to transpose from G up to B♭, a distance of 2 1/2 steps. She just needs to make sure that the other keys are transposed up the same distance.

Then it's just a matter of converting the original chords to Roman numerals, and those Roman numerals to the appropriate chord symbols in the new keys:

Step 4: The first draft

Your chord chart can be simple—with only slashes underneath the chord symbols—or it can be more complex—with rhythmic notation, top-note voicing, or even entire piano voicings notated. Before you put pencil to paper on your first draft, consider how simple or complex you'd like your chart to be. Make a mental note of any signature licks, rhythmic patterns, or chord voicings you want to include, particularly if they'll require the use of more than one staff.

> Brandi wants her chord chart to be easy for the piano player to follow, but she also wants to include signature parts of the song, with chord changes written out in rhythmic notation. Before copying the introduction from the sheet music, she goes to the piano and pounds out the melody notes of the introduction, listening carefully.

Hard Heart to Break

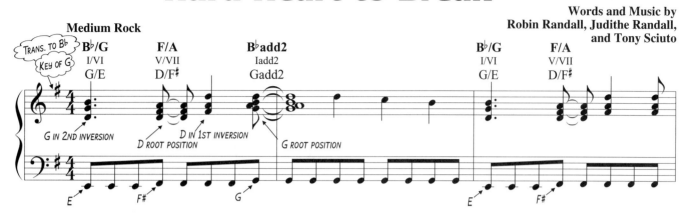

Words and Music by
Robin Randall, Judithe Randall,
and Tony Sciuto

Once she recognizes the notes of the guitar riff, she knows that she can safely copy the introduction from the sheet music and have the guitar riff included. She makes a mental note that she will begin the chart in two staves, for the distinctive intro, but will use only one staff per line in the rest of the chart.

Begin your first draft by transfering the information from the top of your Form Analysis Chart to the top of your lead sheet or chord chart.

MID-TEMPO ROCK AS RECORDED BY DIANA DEWITT

HARD HEART TO BREAK

WORDS & MUSIC BY ROBIN RANDALL, JUDITHE RANDALL, AND TONY SCIUTO

Then, referring to Form Analysis portion of your chart and the Road Map you constructed, block out the entire song in bars.

Take it one step at a time on your first draft. Notice, for instance, if chords change on the upbeat in a certain section—you should probably use rhythmic notation there. Is there a particularly tough melody note the singer might not hit? Consider including that pitch in the accompaniment and using top-note voicing. Remember to add word cues in your chord chart, where appropriate.

Starting with section A of her sheet music, Brandi looks at the first bar and notices that the chord changes on a downbeat. She transfers the chords on her sheet music to her chord chart and puts slashes underneath the chord symbols to indicate where chord changes occur.

In the fourth bar of the prechorus, Brandi sees a chord change on the upbeat of beat 3. She knows that she must use rhythmic notation in her chord chart to indicate when chords are syncopated and change before the downbeat.

Brandi goes through the entire sheet music, section by section, transferring the chord symbols onto her chord chart using slashes and rhythmic notation. Occasionally, she considers using top-note voicing to support and strengthen a melody line. For example, on the recording, the melody line has a chord change on the upbeats of beats 2 and 4 in section C of the song:

When you've finished your first draft, draw boxes around the signs so that the symbols and terms stand out, and add small arrows from the boxes to help direct the musicians who'll be reading your chart.

MID-TEMPO ROCK AS RECORDED BY DIANA DEWITT

HARD HEART TO BREAK

WORDS & MUSIC BY ROBIN RANDALL, JUDITHE RANDALL, AND TONY SCIUTO

72

Step 5: The final draft

Whew! Your work is just about done. Before beginning your final draft, though, make sure to check your first draft by asking yourself a series of questions:

- Did I include a style description and authors' names?
- Did I remember to include a time signature, metronome indication, and key signature?
- Did I indicate odd-numbered measures and/or key changes?
- Did I accidentally skip any measures when transferring?
- Did I number the measures (or every few measures)?
- Are my chord symbols easy to read? Did I forget any?
- Are the chords placed in the correct measures and over the correct beats?
- Do the slashes line up with the chord symbols?
- Do I need additional rhythmic notation, or are slashes sufficient?
- Did I forget any Road Signs, such as D.S. al Coda or repeat brackets?
- Are the Road Signs correctly placed and easy to find?
- Are my rehearsal letters correctly placed? Did I forget any?
- Do I need dynamics? If so, where should they go?
- Are there any Road Indicators I should include? (Are there any places the music slows down, stops, or resumes?)
- Did I include word cues? Do they match the correct musical measures?
- Is my bar placement well-spaced? How is my spacing in general?
- Is my chart easy to read and follow? (Are the note stems and beams straight? Are they going in the correct direction? Are the clefs readable? And so on.)

If you're satisfied with your answers here, you're ready to start your final draft.

For a sharper and cleaner looking final draft, I suggest recopying the chart entirely, in ink. Though you could simply ink over your first draft to create a final copy, you're really better off starting fresh. Remember: Neatness now pays off later in the form of a better performance of your song. When you're done, always make one photocopy of the chart for yourself—as a backup copy, in case something happens to your original—and then make any additional photocopies for the musicians who'll be playing from it.

Incidentally, on each copy you give out, I suggest you highlight important symbols and indicators with a colored highlighting pen. (Don't highlight your original or backup copy, however, because you may need to make more copies later, and the highlighted areas will appear dark gray and be harder to read when photocopied.) You might even decide to use two different color highlighters to call attention to different sections—but be careful not to over-highlight or use more than two colors, because too much color is distracting and defeats the purpose of highlighting.

Brandi Meets Barry at the Beach

Squishing his toes in the sand, Barry stared idly at the beach babes. They didn't have babes like this back in Hoboken. Like a kid in a candy store, he felt overwhelmed by the selection. Then he saw her—a Babe Ruth among the Good 'n' Plenty. He couldn't believe his eyes. She had risen from the waves and was heading toward him, carrying her surfboard, "Surfboard Queen of Idaho" painted on one side.

It had to be fate. Her towel was right in front of his. He couldn't let this opportunity pass. He had to at least try to meet her... but how? He racked his brain. She hadn't even noticed him; she was already reading a book. Wait a minute, that was his in—he'd talk to her about the book! If only he could see the cover... He leaned closer and closer. He could smell the coconut oil on her skin, but without his glasses, the title was a blur. He leaned closer still.

"Excuse me?" Big blue eyes stared at him.

"Oh... uh... You looked so into that book. I wanted to know what it was."

She showed him the cover, which read, "A Step-by-Step Guide to Writing Lead Sheets and Chord Charts."

"So, you're a musician!"

"I'm a singer."

"Hey that's great. I'm a songwriter. Do you write music too?"

"No, but I just finished my first chord chart."

"By following that handy-dandy guide?"

"Yeah, I think it came out pretty good, too. I'm going to use it for my audition with 'Celebrity Search' next week."

"Wow! 'Celebrity Search.' That's great. What song are you gonna sing?"

"'Hard Heart to Break.'"

"Never heard of it. Why'd you pick that song?"

"Because I like it, and I can sing it well."

"Sing it to me."

Brandi sang a chorus.

"That's a cool song... but I don't think it's really you. What I mean is... the way you bounded out of the surf..."

"You were watching me?"

"I couldn't take my eyes off you. You're so... so energetic... so dynamic. That song is so serious. You seem like someone who enjoys life, who wants to have a good time. You need a song that's more upbeat. Hey, I could write a song for you..."

"Whoa, cowboy! I've already got a song, and I just finished my chord chart."

"But this would be tailor made for you. Gimme a chance. I could write a great song. And, if you don't like it, you don't have to use it. What have you got to lose?"

"Nothing, I guess. But you don't even know my vocal range. How do you know what key to put it in?"

"What's your range?"

"Two octaves from low G. And I sing better on the upper notes of the staff."

"Uh… whatever."

"Hey, I need the song by Thursday—my audition is Saturday afternoon. I need a couple of days to rehearse. And, it has to be in chord chart form. Oh wait, the melody has to be there too—so I guess I need a lead sheet, not a chord chart. Can you write a lead sheet?"

"Well… yeah… but I'm kinda slow."

"Here… You can use my book."

"I don't think a book is going to make me any faster. It'll probably slow me down, since I'll have to stop and read it when I could be working on my song."

"No… it's a guide… step-by-step. Give it a try."

"OK. Maybe it'll help me with the 'upper notes of the staff' stuff, too."

"It will."

"Can I get your name and number?"

"It's all on the inside cover. I still don't know how you can write a song for someone you just met."

"I know you like to surf."

Chapter Ten

10 ORIGINAL SONG → LEAD SHEET

Barry has written an original song for Brandi, and he wants to have a demo of it recorded by some professional musicians. Of course, he could just hand the musicians his own rough recording and have them figure out the tune, but that would take them time and cost Barry money. Also, if his rough recording contained wrong notes, they would probably show up on the finished demo. On the other hand, if he provides the musicians with a lead sheet—with the melody, chords, and lyrics clearly written out—he can bypass all of these problems.

In this chapter, we'll learn how to create a lead sheet for an original song. The process is really quite similar to creating a lead sheet or chord chart from sheet music, but the preparation required is more extensive, because this time it's up to us to figure out all the musical details—the lyrics, chords, melody, rhythms, etc. Our working example will be Barry's new song, "The Surfboard Queen of Idaho." Because we'll be creating a lead sheet (not a chord chart) for "Surfboard Queen," the emphasis here will be on notating *melody*. You'll find this method useful for transcribing any melody, original or otherwise.

Step 1: The lyric sheet

With no sheet music to fall back on, we'll need something to serve as a visual guide for laying out our lead sheet—something to help us determine the song's form and to prepare us for notating its melody. This is where the lyric sheet comes in. To make the lyric sheet really work for us, we'll need to do two things:

1. Group the lyrics by section (verse, chorus, etc.)

2. Divide each section into measures

Take a few listens to Barry's song "The Surfboard Queen of Idaho," paying attention to the section changes—verses, choruses, etc. When you feel somewhat comfortable with the tune, write out its lyrics, grouping them by section.

70 The Surfboard Queen of Idaho

Verse 1	I'm wearing my bikini And I'm ready to go But I'm stuck in the state where Potatoes grow
Pre-Chorus 1	Sure I've got a boyfriend His name is Fred But do I want to marry Mr. Potato Head?
Chorus 1	Where I live salty breezes don't blow The only waves we get come from the radio I've got my surfboard and nowhere to go I'm the Surfboard Queen of Idaho

Verse 2	I'm drivin' my old Woody
	I don't get very far
	Yes I have a tan, but
	It's from a jar

Pre-Chorus 2	As for my silly girlfriends
	They just don't care
	When I talk of a big wave
	They're lookin' at my hair.

Chorus 2	(Repeat Chorus)

Bridge	I've been so unhappy for so many years
	I've got potatoes growing outta my ears
	If only I could get my potatoes cashed
	But my mom's brains are fried and my dad's are mashed.

Verse 3	Won't someone send a ticket
	To take me up and away
	I wanna learn to party
	Like they do in L.A.

Pre-Chorus 3	Everyone around here
	Is a real live dope
	When I say "Let's hang ten."
	They get out the rope.

Chorus 3	(Repeat Chorus)

Next, start inserting barlines. The process of inserting barlines—determining which syllables of a lyric occur with which beats of the melody—is called *scansion*. The key to scansion is listening for the accented syllables of the lyric. Sing the lyric aloud, line by line, keeping a constant tempo, and listen for the stressed syllables in each line.

> I'm wear-ing my bi-**ki**-ni
> And I'm read-y to **go**
> But I'm stuck in the **state** where
> Po-ta-toes **grow**…

The syllables you hear as accented or stressed will be either downbeats or anticipations of downbeats (the upbeat of a previous measure), either of which should be marked with a barline.

The downbeat of a measure might also fall on a rest; there can be silence on a downbeat. This is the case in this first verse of "Surfboard Queen"—where there is a quarter rest (or more) before the start of each line. These rests mark the downbeats of new measures, so barlines should be inserted at the start of each of these lines as well.

> /I'm wearing my bi/**kini**
> /And I'm ready to /**go**
> /But I'm stuck in the /**state** where
> /Potatoes /**grow**…

Keep in mind, an accented syllable does not *always* signal the start of a new measure—particularly if the song is in 4/4 time. There may be *secondary* accents that stick out to your ear:

/I'm *wearing* my bi/**ki**ni
/And I'm *ready* to /**go**
/But I'm *stuck* in the /**state** where
/Po*ta*toes /**grow**…

These secondary accents are worth noticing, but they don't signal the start of a new measure—just the middle of a 4/4 measure. Listen for the *primary* accents when inserting barlines.

It is usually helpful to look at the printed lyric while you listen to a recording, especially with mid- to up-tempo songs where the lines are sung quickly. Say each line aloud, and ask yourself, "Which syllable or word stands out?" Tapping out the tempo in a steady quarter-note pulse while saying or singing the lyric also helps.

Some Additional Tips

• Usually the accented syllable of a word coincides with an accented beat. Knowing this can help you divide up a lyric sheet into measures. For example, Barry's first line, "I'm wearing my bikini," could have been accented seven different ways:

I'm wear-ing my bi-ki-ni
I'm *wear*-ing my bi-ki-ni
I'm wear-*ing* my bi-ki-ni
I'm wear-ing *my* bi-ki-ni
I'm wear-ing my *bi*-ki-ni
I'm wear-ing my bi-*ki*-ni
I'm wear-ing my bi-ki-*ni*

Some of these accents would sound better than others, because some sound more like everyday conversation. Of the above examples, 1, 2, 4, and 6 sound fine; the others sound peculiar. (Of course, Barry could have chosen a peculiar accent, like the "ing" of "wearing"; songwriters sometimes do this.)

• Often, the word directly in front of the downbeat is a short word such as "to," "the," "a," "and," "but," "I've," or "you." Syllables prior to accented syllables are pickups from the previous measures. In our example, the entire first half of each line is a pickup into the next downbeat.

PICKUPS	DOWNBEATS
I'm wear-ing my bi-	**ki**-ni
And I'm read-y to	**go**
But I'm stuck in the	**state** where
Po-ta-toes	**grow**

• Occasionally, songs have odd-metered bars, such as a 2/4 bar inserted in a song that is primarily in 4/4 time. These are infrequent, however. If you miss an odd-metered bar, the accented syllables and barlines will be thrown off, and you'll probably notice it.

Here's a complete lyric sheet for "Surfboard Queen" with barlines and measure numbers inserted. Check it against your own version.

The Surfboard Queen of Idaho

4-Bar Intro

Verse 1
| (4)   I'm wearing my bi | (5) kini —|
| (6)   And I'm ready to | go (7) —|
| (8)   But I'm stuck in the state where (9) —|
| (10) Potatoes | grow. (11) —|

Pre-Chorus 1
(12) Sure I've got a	boyfriend (13) —
(14) His name is	Fred (15) —
(16) But do I want to	marry (17) —
(18) Mr. Potato Head? (19) —	(20) *Rests* —

Chorus 1
| (21) Where I live salty | breezes don't blow (22) —|
| (23) The only waves we get come from the | radio (24) —
       I've | (25) got my surfboard and | nowhere to go (26) —
       I'm the | (27) Surfboard Queen of | Ida (28) | ho. (29) —|

Verse 2
(30) I'm drivin' my old	Woody (31) —
(32) I don't get very	far (33) —
(34) Yes I have a	tan, but (35) —
(36) It's from a	jar. (37) —

Pre-Chorus 2
(38) As for my silly	girlfriends (39) —
(40) They just don't	care (41) —
(42) When I talk of a	big wave (43)—
(44) They're lookin' at my	hair. (45) —| (46) *Rests* —

Chorus 3   *(Repeat Chorus)* (Bars 47-55)

Bridge
| (56) I've | (57) been so unhappy for | so many years (58)
       I've | (59) got potatoes growing | outta my ears (60)
       If | (61) only I could get my po | tatoes cashed (62)
       But my | (63) mom's brains are fried and my | (64) dad's are mashed.
| (65) *Rests* —|

Verse 3
(66) Won't someone send a	ticket (67) —
(68) To take me up and a	way (69) —
(70) I wanna learn to	party (71) —
(72) Like they do in L.	A. (73) —

Pre-Chorus 3
(74) Everyone a	round here (75) —
(76) Is a real live	dope (77) —
(78) When I say "Let's	hang ten." (79) —
(80) They get out the	rope. (81) —| (82) *Rests* —

Chorus 3   *(Repeat Chorus)* (Bars 83-92)

Tag   (Bars 93-100)

Step 2: The Form Analysis Chart

Even when notating your own song, filling out a Form Analysis Chart is a crucial step. It can help minimize the time you spend transcribing your song and can eliminate the need for more than one rough draft of your lead sheet.

With your lyric sheet as a guide, you should be able to map out your song now, section by section and measure by measure. If you have trouble with any of this (e.g., the key, the melodic range), simply leave it blank, and return to it later. Here's a completed chart for "Surfboard Queen." Take a good look at it.

Form Analysis Chart

Song Title: _SURFBOARD QUEEN OF IDAHO_

Songwriter/Artist: _BARRY_

Key	Time Signature	Tempo	Melodic Range	Style Description
F	4/4	♩=154	HIGH – D ON STAFF LOW – 8b BELOW STAFF	UPTEMPO POP/ROCK W/SURF FEEL

Form of Song			Road Map Instructions	Comments
Song Section	Rehearsal Letters	Number of Bars		
INTRO	—	4	LAST BAR – WRITE "TACET" USE RAILROAD TRACKS //	WRITE OUT INSTR. MELODY
VS 1	A	8	1ST BAR – "A TEMPO" 8TH BAR TACET / RR. TRACKS PUT A REPEAT BRACKET BEFORE BAR 1	
PRE CH 1	B	8	1ST BAR – "A TEMPO" 8TH BAR TACET / R.R. TRACKS	WRITE RHY. NOTATION OF CHORDS – BAR 7
CH. 1	C	10	10TH BAR – 1ST ENDING, PUT REPEAT BRACKET – BACK TO Ⓐ, TACET/ R.R. TRACK / TO CODA AFTER BAR 9	RHY. NOTATION – BAR 9 SHOW MELODY VARIATION
VS 2	A	8	SAME AS VS 1/ REPEAT W/BRACKETS	
PRECH 2	B	8	SAME AS P.C. 1/ "	" " "
CH 2	C	10	SAME AS CH. 1 EXCEPT 10TH BAR MAKE 2ND ENDING USE "TACET"/R.R.T.	LEADS INTO BRIDGE
BR	D	10	END OF SECTION PUT "D.S. AL CODA", LAST BAR // + TACET, PLACE 𝄋 AT BEG. OF Ⓐ	
VS 3	A	8	IS REPEATED (AT 𝄋)	
PRE CH 3	B	8	" " "	
CH 3	C	10	10TH BAR IS 1ST BAR OF CODA AFTER BAR 9 - SKIP TO CODA SECTION	
CODA	E	1+12	LAST BAR OF TAG OF CHORUS = 3x STARTS CODA	REPEAT TAG USING REP. BRACKETS W/1ST + 2ND ENDINGS

Additional Notes: ABC TWICE (ABOVE) IS THE SAME /10TH BAR OF Ⓒ
CAN CONDENSE AS = 𝄆: A B C:𝄇 USE ⌐(1)————:𝄇⌐(2)————
D (BR) MUST WRITE OUT   DIFFERENT ENDINGS
ABC AGAIN – SAME GROUP – USE D.S.
TAG MUST WRITE OUT – CALL IT Ⓔ

Step 3: The key

Evaluating the key of your song should be a fairly quick process. If you haven't already done so, play through the song's melody or chords, and either listen for the tonic note/chord or match the component notes of the song to a scale in the Transposition Chart. If, later on, you find you've misidentified the key, you can always fix this on the final draft.

Now's also the time to consider things like melodic range and accompaniment instrumentation. Will the singer be able to hit all the notes in this key? Will the band sound their best? Again, you can change your mind once you've completed your first draft. Refer to Chapter 7 if you need help transposing.

Step 4: The first draft

Now you're ready to begin notating the melody. First, write out the lyrics again, but on staff paper. Depending on the number of words or syllables in each bar, you should be able to fit two to four bars of the lyric underneath each staff. You don't want to crowd the lyric—this will be the start of your rough draft.

Place a barline at the start of each new measure and a double barline at the end of each musical section. If the song begins with a pickup measure, place a double barline after the pickup to show the start of the musical verse. In Barry's song, for example, "I'm wearing my bikini" is the start of the lyric, but "...ki-ni" is the start of the musical verse, because it is where the first downbeat occurs:

Divide the lyric into syllables, hyphenating those words with more than one syllable. Wherever a melody note is to be held out, write a line after that word. The length of the line should be representative of the note's duration.

Do not write out the lyrics to second or third verses and choruses if they are musically identical to an earlier section. Instead, use Road Map symbols to indicate these repeated sections.

As an additional preparation, you might choose to write a rhythm count above each staff line, aligning each beat number with its corresponding syllable or word. You'll have to estimate the beat placement, because you won't know how the beats will align with the syllables until the melody has been rhythmically notated on the staff.

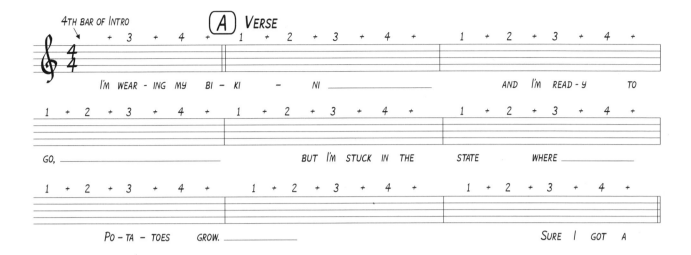

At this point, make a photocopy of your work, so that you won't have to copy it over when you convert from rhythmic notation to melody notes.

Next, apply rhythmic notation to your lyric.

Tap out a slow, steady pulse with your right or left hand, and count out the meter of your song (e.g., "One-and, two-and, three-and, four-and") as you tap. Every time your hand comes down, it is a beat. Every time your hand comes up, it is an "and" between the beats.

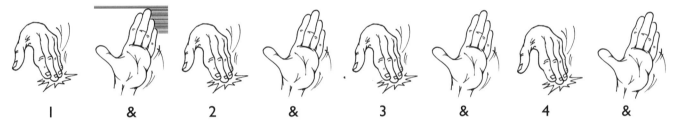

Once you're comfortable with the rhythm, replace each beat number or "and" with a syllable of the lyric (or with silence, if appropriate). When you can tap and count out a phrase or song section like this, notate it using rhythmic notation symbols.

Work through each phrase and section, until the entire melody is rhythmically notated. Here are the first two sections of "Surfboard Queen" in rhythmic notation:

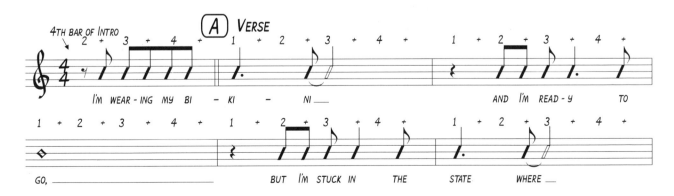

83

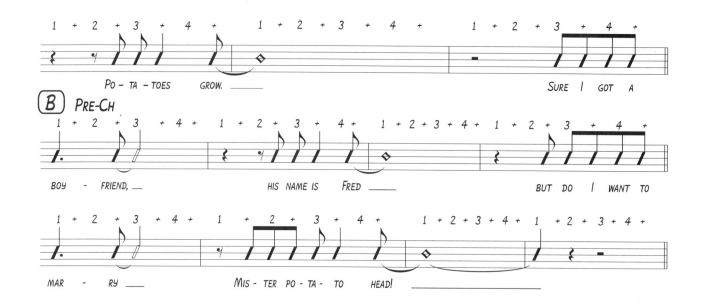

- Pay attention to whether syllables fall on the downbeats (1, 2, 3, and 4) or the upbeats (the "and"s)—some accented syllables fall on upbeats and extend into the following downbeats. This is called *syncopation*, and it is extremely common in popular music.

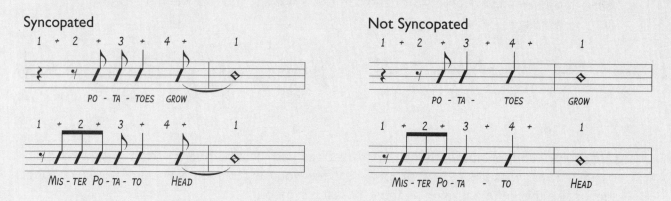

(Some syllables might fall in-between the downbeats and upbeats, which will require the use of sixteenth notes. "Surfboard Queen," however, contains no sixteenth notes.)

- Sometimes a syllable lasts longer than one beat. For example, in one part of "Surfboard Queen," the first syllable of "I-da-ho" lasts three beats. In addition, the three beats of this syllable are subdivided into eighth notes, because the melody uses more than one note for this syllable. This is called a *melisma* and is indicated with a slur.

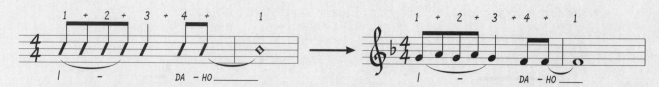

The rhythmic notation does not show the different tones contained in the long "I" syllable, but once this notation is replaced with melody notes, the tone variation will become clear.

- Try singing or speaking the lyric along with a metronome or a drum machine click, so that you can concentrate on the rhythm of the lyric. Also, don't be afraid to *slow down* your tempo if it helps you to isolate a rhythm.

Finally, convert each rhythmic symbol into a melody note.

Beginning with the very first measure of your song, sing each note aloud, and match its pitch on your instrument. Once you've determined a pitch, you can find its rhythmic value on your rhythm notation and then draw the complete note on the "lyrics only" photocopy you made previously.

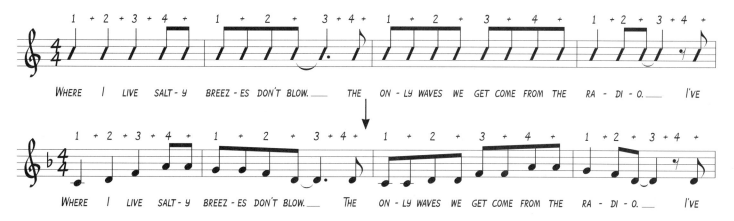

Go through your song, measure by measure, singing the melody and lyrics and playing the chords on a piano. To keep track of which chords go with which measures, write the chord symbols above the staff as you goes along.

Pop Rock (in the "Surf Music of the '60s" Tradition)

SURFBOARD QUEEN OF IDAHO

Words & Music by Barry

Step 5: The final draft

Before you begin your final draft of this lead sheet, ask yourself the same questions you asked when you created a chord chart from sheet music. (See p. 74.) If you're satisfied with your answers to these questions—and with your rough draft—recopy the lead sheet in ink.

Don't forget, when making photocopies of your final draft, keep one as a backup copy along with your original, and then highlight important symbols and indicators on the copies that you give out to other musicians.

Getting a Demo Done Faster

"Hello?"

"Hi. My name's Barry. I'm calling about your ad in *The Music Connection.*"

"Yeah…"

"It says that you can make a demo of my song."

"Sure."

"It's a really rockin' tune, and I need a really great guitar player. Are you a great guitar player?"

"Yeah."

"I'm trying to impress this singer, so I need the recording to sound really… BIG."

"Big?"

"Yeah, you know, professional… polished. It's for 'Celebrity Search.'"

"So you want more than a guitar player."

"Yeah, I want the full band sound for her backing track."

"OK, I can do that. When do you need it?"

"Thursday."

"Thursday! This is Tuesday. How am I supposed to learn a song and record it that fast?"

"I have a lead sheet. You can read music, can't you?"

"I'm OK with chords… a lead sheet will help. Can you sing it onto a cassette for me too?"

"Yeah. No problem."

"Thursday's cool then. Can you bring it by?"

"Sure. How about four?"

"Great."

A Better Way to Teach Songs

"Come in! Door's open."

Barry could hear his song playing in another room.

"I'm in here! I'm making a tape copy."

Barry followed the voice. Bo was setting the levels on the tape machine.

"It sounds good! I hope Brandi's impressed."

"Brandi?"

"She's the 'Surfboard Queen.'"

"Oh, yeah."

"How was the lead sheet? Could you follow it OK?"

"Yeah, it really saved me some time in figuring out the chords and how the song goes. Actually, I front this cover band on the weekends, and if I could take down some tunes on paper, it'd really save time teaching my band the songs."

"How do you teach them the songs now?"

"By ear. I just keep playing it over and over until they get it. I'd lift it off the recording, but I'm pretty slow, and it looks messy—hard to read."

"I'll lend you this book I used to make my lead sheet. I'm sure it'll help. It has a chapter on transcribing from recordings."

"OK, I'll give it a try."

"Well, here's your money. Thanks for the track. I'm gonna run it over to Brandi."

Chapter Eleven

RECORDING → CHORD CHART

As singers and musicians, we can't always find sheet music for the songs that we want to perform, so we need to be able to transcribe, or "take down," songs from recordings. In this chapter, we'll learn how to do just that, step by step. One word of caution here: this type of transcription is not easy. When attempting your first few songs, take things slowly; otherwise, taking a song apart can seem like an overwhelming task. With practice, transcribing will become much easier; you'll learn to recognize common chord progressions, rhythms, and melodic patterns. But when first learning to transcribe, start with simple songs with few chord changes. Many country, rock, and "doo-wop" tunes fit into this category.

Our working example will be "Where Are You Now?," a song that Bo wants to transcribe for his band. Because we'll be creating a chord chart (not a lead sheet), the emphasis here will be on figuring out chords. You should find this method useful for songs of all types.

Step 1: The lyric sheet

Again, because we have no sheet music to refer to, we'll need to create a lyric sheet to start the transcription process. A lyric sheet will help us out not only initially, when we're laying out our chord chart, but also later on, when we need to add word cues.

 Take a few listens to "Where Are You Know?," and write out its lyrics, section by section.

	Intro	
Verse I	City streets, walking after midnight Lost in the crowd, out on my own Without you here, the nights are never-ending I still see your face wherever I go	**A**
Pre-Chorus I	I close my eyes across a million miles of broken dreams And pray your restless soul Will lead you back again to me Back again to me	
Chorus I	Where are you now? Are you missing me tonight? Or does someone else hold you tight? Baby, look around Are you just too blind to see No one could love you more than me	**B**
Tag I	And when your world comes tumbling down Someday I'll hear you say "Where are you now?"	

→ *Re-Intro*

Verse 2	All alone in a town full of strangers Talking to myself over a drink or two Looking through tears for a runaway angel Dancing till dawn with memories of you	**A**
Pre-Chorus 2	I listen to my lonely heart In rhythm with the rain And pray I'll find a way To make your stormy seasons change, baby	
Chorus 2	*(Repeat Chorus and Tag)*	**B**
Bridge	I wonder if you ever wonder what became of me Baby, I need you so desperately tonight Tonight Where are you now?	**C**
Gtr. Solo/Ch. 3	*Re-Intro/Gtr. Solo over Chorus*	**B**
Tag 3	And when your world comes tumbling down Someday I'll hear you say, I know I'll hear you say	
Chorus 4	*(Repeat Chorus)*	**B**
Chorus Vamp	*(Ad-lib vocals over Chorus)*	**B**

Step 2: The Form Analysis Chart

On first listening to a piece of music, you might think you have a lot of material to transcribe; however, most songs are repetitious. By filling out a Form Analysis Chart, you can break a song down into its basic elements and see those repetitions.

Once you've transcribed the lyrics to your song, you're ready to start a Form Analysis Chart.

- Determine the style of the song. Is it a "fast rocker"? A "slow ballad"? A "mid-tempo blues"? Does the accompaniment have a distinctive, characteristic sound? Indicate this in the Style Description column.

- List the song sections (Intro, Verse, Chorus, etc.), label each with a rehearsal letter, and then determine the number of measures in each by listening to the audio again. Decide where you'll place double bars in the score. Is the "set-up" section to the chorus enough of a musical statement to warrant a new rehearsal letter label? (If not, you must group it as part of the verse and begin the chorus with a double bar.)

- Note any tempo changes, breaks, or modulations in the song. If you can't tell exactly where a song modulates, simply write "key change" in the Comments column. (Later, you can figure out how and where the key change occured.)

- Listen to the song several times, each time concentrating on a different aspect of the tune— first the melody and lyrics, then the guitar, then the bass, the drums, and so on. Decide if your chord chart should be just a slash chart with occasional lyric cues, or if it should include other instrumental parts. How important is the bass line? Is it a signature bass part that adds a recognizable quality to the song, or can it be dictated by word description alone? Should a guitar or synth part be added, or can slashes be used with key descriptive words such as "play arpeggios," "gtr-choke," or "staccato"?

Complete a Form Analysis Chart for "Where Are You Now?," and then compare it to Bo's below:

Form Analysis Chart

Song Title: _WHERE ARE YOU NOW?_

Songwriter/Artist: _ROBIN RANDALL, JUDITH RANDALL, JUNO ROXAS, JAMES CHRISTIAN_

Key	Time Signature	Tempo	Melodic Range	Style Description
Eb	4/4	♩=90	Eb BELOW MID C TO C ABOVE MID C RANGE: MINOR 10TH	MID-TEMPO POP/ROCK BALLAD w/8TH NOTE FEEL

Song Section	Rehearsal Letters	Number of Bars	Road Map Instructions	Comments
INTRO	—	4	DISTINCTIVE SIGNATURE GTR/KB MELODY LINE	
VERSE 1	A	8	GTR PLAYS 8THS PLAYED TWICE/BASS WHOLE NOTES (SPARSE W/FILLS)	
PRE-CH 1	B	5	GTR COL BASS LINE	
CH 1	C	8+6	1ST 8 BARS - KICK DRUM IN LAST 6 BARS - FULL DRUMS IN (TAG)	
RE-INTRO	—	2	½ OF INTRO	WRITE OUT MELODY LINE
VS 2	A	8	ALL BAND IS IN ———	BASS + GTR: PLAY 8THS
PRE-CH 2	B	4	SAME AS BEFORE, BUT DELETE LAST BAR (MAKE 1ST & 2ND ENDINGS AFTER CH)	
CH 2	C	8+6	FULL GROOVE THROUGH CHORUS	
BRIDGE	D	8	8TH FEEL W/ ♩♫♩ RHYTHM ACCENT	KEY CHANGE
RE-INTRO	—	4	SAME GTR RIFF AS BEFORE PLAYED TWICE	KEY CHANGE 2ND TIME
INSTR. CH	E	8	(4+4) GTR SOLO/CHORUS GROOVE	
TAG OF CH.	F	6	VOCAL IN LAST 6 BARS OF CHORUS	
OUT-CH	G	8	(4+4) 4 BAR VAMP REPEATED	CUE ENDING

Additional Notes: _CAN CONDENSE SONG BY PUTTING REPEAT BRACKETS AROUND SECTIONS A B C W/ 1ST & 2ND ENDINGS. ON SECTION [B], PRE-CH: 5 BARS 1ST TIME/4 BARS 2ND TIME USE 1ST & 2ND ENDINGS._

Step 3: The key

The best way to determine a song's key is to *sing its bass line* and then *match those notes on your instrument.* I suggest using a piano for this, but any instrument with which you're comfortable will work. A bass/treble control or an equilization panel on your tape recorder or stereo is also a helpful tool in this step, because it is usually easier to hear the bass line when the treble is turned down and the bass is turned up.

In addition to listening for the bassline, you can try listening to *the melody* of your song. Generally speaking, a "bright" or "happy" melody suggests that the song is in a major key, while a "dark" or "sad" one suggests the song is in minor. Which major or minor key a song is in can be determined by finding the scale that is running through the melody. A major or minor scale is usually made up of seven notes, and—while a melody *may* contain accidentals—the notes of a melody usually belong to an identifiable major or minor scale.

To figure out the key of "Where Are You Now?," Bo concentrates on the guitar lick in the introduction and sounds out the notes of its melody.

Referring to the Transposition Chart, he sees that this lick could be in either E♭ major or A♭ major—because both keys contain the notes B♭, E♭, A♭, G, and C.

To eliminate one key or the other, Bo tries out the remaining notes of each key. He finds that a D sounds better with the notes of the intro than D♭—so the key must be E♭ major.

Step 4: The first draft

Once you've determined the song's key, work on finding the chord progression for each section.

- Begin by listening for a recognizable harmonic pattern, such as the I-IV-V progression found in "La Bamba" or "Twist and Shout." There is a table of common chord progressions in the appendix of this book. Take some time to become familiar with it. If you can recognize a familiar progression, you don't have to hunt down each chord individually.

- Next, listen for the quality of each chord. Is it major, minor, or dominant? (These three are your only choices diatonically, except for the diminished chord, which is rare in popular music.) If the chord is major, it is likely either a I, IV, or V chord; if minor, it is likely a ii, iii, or vi chord.

- Listen to the bass line for clues. In any given key, there are only seven notes that could make up a diatonic bass melody and seven root position chords that could accompany those bass notes. Any notes other than these would be chromatic and would result in an altered chord.

For example, if a song is in F major, and its second chord has a G in the bass, then that second chord could be a root position Gm (ii) chord:

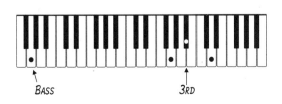

Or it could be a root position G (II) chord, an altered chord outside the key:

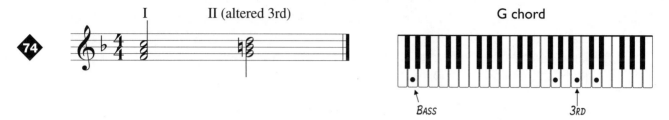

(If you find altered chords in a major key, check to see if they have been borrowed from the parallel minor. This may lead you to identifying more chords in the song.)

However, it might also be a **chord inversion**—like C/G—or a **polychord**—the root of one chord in the bass with an entirely different chord played above it—like D/G:

Or the bass line might work as a "pedal point"; the bass note is fixed, while chords above it change—like this example in C:

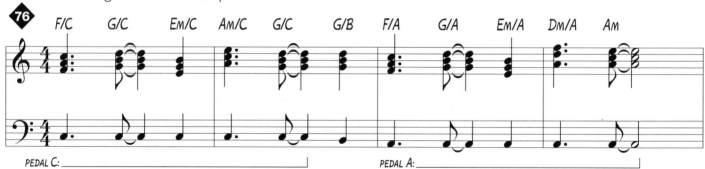

- Finally, consider the vocal melody. Usually, the correct chord contains notes that correspond to notes of the melody, because they are all part of a single harmony. Without any common notes between them, the melody and accompaniment would sound unusually dissonant. Therefore, it is a good idea to first determine if the vocal melody is the root, third, or fifth of the chord. For example, a C note in the vocal melody could be the root of C, the third of Am or A♭, or the fifth of F or Fm.

If none of these fit, then the C could be an upper extension of the chord, such as the seventh of a Dm7, the ninth of a B♭maj9, the eleventh of a Gm11, or the thirteenth of an E♭13 chord, and so on. If a melody note is one of the notes of a basic triad, the harmony will sound basic and simple. If it is an extension, the higher the extension—9th, 11th, 7th—the more sophisticated and dissonant the sound.

Bo listens to the bass notes in the introduction of "Where Are You Now?" He hears a C note on beat 1 that changes to an A♭ on beat 3. This is followed by a B♭ on the upbeat of beat 4.

The first chord sounds like a minor one to Bo. Since there is a C in the bass, he plays Cm, which sounds correct and harmonizes with the vocal melody. (He also tries C major, but this doesn't sound right.) Once Bo has determined that his first chord is Cm, he looks at the next two bass notes, A♭ and B♭, and figures out these chords in a similar manner. As it turns out, all of the first notes of the bass line are roots of first position chords diatonic to the key of E♭ major.

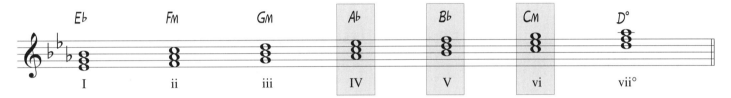

As you figure out the chords, block out a sketch of the measures for each section, and add slashes or rhythmic notation to each measure to keep track of the beats. Look at your Form Analysis Chart for the number of measures in a section, the rehearsal letters, and any other important information.

Here's the introduction of "Where Are You Now?" with the bass line and guitar/piano melodies notated and the measures blocked out.

Write lyric cues at the beginning of each measure, or at least at the beginning and end of each song section, to help the musicians keep their place in the chart. Also, look for sections that can be condensed with simile marks or repeats signs.

Bo listens to the bass line in the verse several times and then to the qualities of each chord to decide whether they are major or minor. He determines the chord progression in this section to be E♭sus2–B♭/G–A♭sus2–B♭sus4–B♭. He realizes that these four bars of music repeat, so to save space on his final draft, he uses a "simile" sign to condense the eight bars into four.

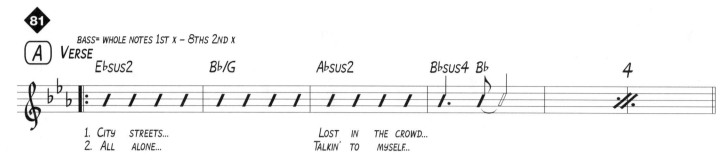

In the next section, the pre-chorus, Bo finds a G major chord. He realizes that this is an altered chord in the key of E♭ major because it is major instead of minor—a III instead of a iii. (In fact, it's a secondary dominant chord, because it functions as the dominant of the following chord, Cm.) Later in the pre-chorus, he finds another altered chord: the bass contains a D♭, which is the flat-7th scale degree of E♭, while the guitar/piano voicing forms an A♭maj7 chord. Bo decides he has a polychord on his hands, which he labels A♭maj7/D♭.

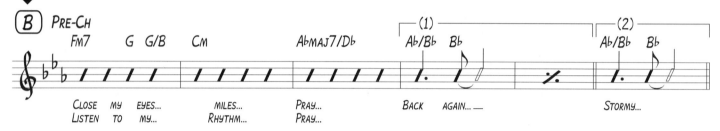

Bo goes through the entire song, section by section, listening to the bass line and chord qualities, figuring out the chords and chord progressions. He must listen to each section of the song many times. The chorus is a four-bar chord progression: one measure of E♭ (I), one meas-ure of Cm (vi), one measure of A♭sus2 (IV), two beats of C♭ (♭VI) altered, and two beats of D♭ (♭VII) altered. This four-bar chord progression repeats, so Bo notates his chart this way:

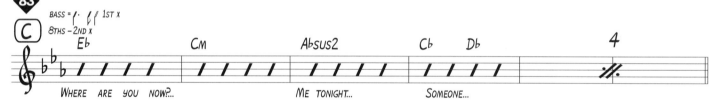

Also, on his Form Analysis Chart, Bo notes the bass pattern: (♩. ♪ ♪) for the chorus, and that the bass plays eighth notes in measure 9, which is a tag added to a regular eight-bar chorus. The chord progression for measure 9 (the tag) is: one measure of Fm7 (ii), one measure of Gm7#5 (iii), one measure of A♭ (IV), one measure of A♭sus2/C (IV/III), B♭ (V), and A♭/F (IV/II). Bo notes the rhythmic notation of this last bar:

Notice the A♭/F (IV/II) ties over into the next bar, followed by A♭/B♭ (IV/V), then into the first ending, which is the reintroduction:

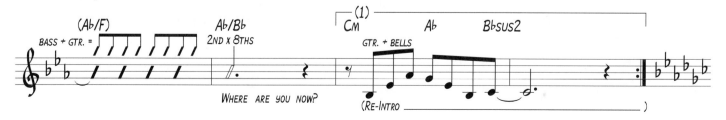

Also, watch out for key changes, which will most likely occur at the start of a new section.

The second ending of the chorus begins the bridge. Bo hears the bass playing eighth notes and, while figuring out the bass line, realizes that the key has changed. It is no longer E♭, because the first measure of the bridge is C♭, and the second is D♭, neither of which belong to the key. From looking at his Transposition Chart, Bo sees that C♭ and D♭ are diatonic to the key of G♭ major:

	I	ii	iii	IV	V	vi	vii°
Key of E♭ Major:	E♭	F	G	A♭	B♭	C	D
Key of G♭ major:	G♭	A♭	B♭	C♭	D♭	E♭	F

So he places a G♭ key signature at the start of the bridge and a direction for the bass to play eighths. The bridge section looks like this when he is done:

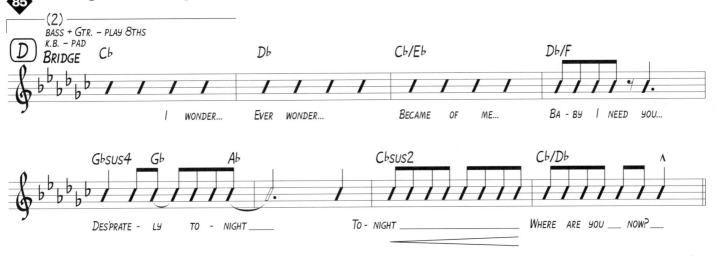

After the bridge, Bo hears a reintro—two measures in G♭ and two in E♭—so he notes a key change in the third measure.

The re-intro is followed by Section E, the guitar solo, which is identical to the first eight measures of the chorus (4 measures + 4 measures):

This instrumental part is followed by a return to vocals, identical to the last six measures of the chorus, the tag. The only difference is that the sixth measure builds dynamically, leading into the chorus (Section G). For even spacing, Bo divides this six-bar section into three measures per staff line.

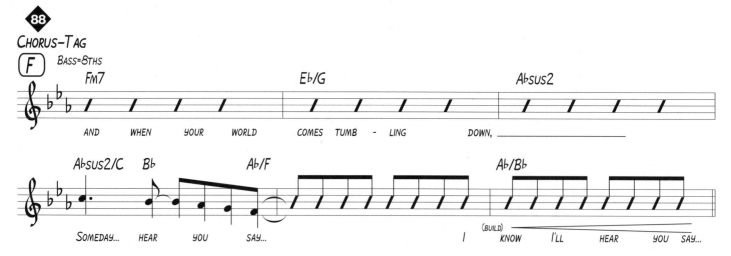

Finally, consider how you'll end your song. If the recording ends in a fade-out, you'll probably want to rethink the ending for a live performance.

The final section of "Where Are You Now?" is a vamp on the chorus—the first four bars of the chorus repeat as the song fades out. Since fading out on stage is anticlimactic and hard to control, Bo writes "Vamp till cued" and an ending that uses the introduction.

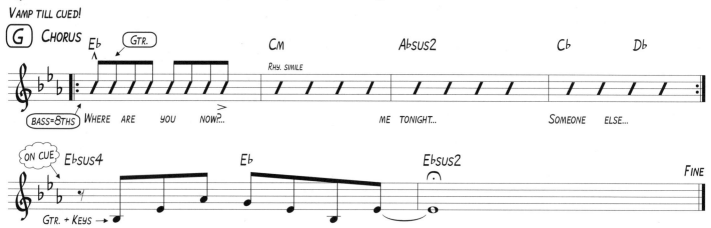

Another viable option would have been to have the first four bars of the chorus repeat a specific number of times—e.g., "Play 6x."

Step 5: The final draft

You may find yourself listening to each song section many, many times in order to figure out its chords. Don't worry, that's normal. Once you've completed the first draft of your trans-cription, ask yourself the following questions, and then recopy the chart in ink.

- How many pages will the chart be?
- How many bars per line should be used?
- Should the form, arrangement, or length of the song be changed?
- What sections can be repeated using Road Map symbols? What sections must be written out?
- How many endings are needed to repeat back to a section or to go on to the next?
- Does the song have a tag or a vamp? How will it end?
- Are all important Road Indicators included?
- If there is a key change, is it marked with a key signature change at the start of the section?

Once again, when you've finished your final draft, make one photocopy as a backup, and then make additional photocopies for any musicians who'll be reading the chart. Highlight any important indicators on these copies with a colored highlighting pen.

Mid-Tempo Pop/Rock Ballad

Where Are You Now?

Words & Music by Robin Randall, Judithe Randall, and Juno Roxas

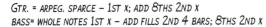

GTR. = ARPEG. SPARCE – 1ST X; ADD 8THS 2ND X
BASS= WHOLE NOTES 1ST X – ADD FILLS 2ND 4 BARS; 8THS 2ND X

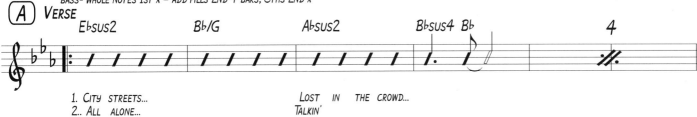

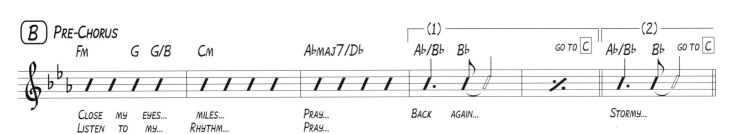

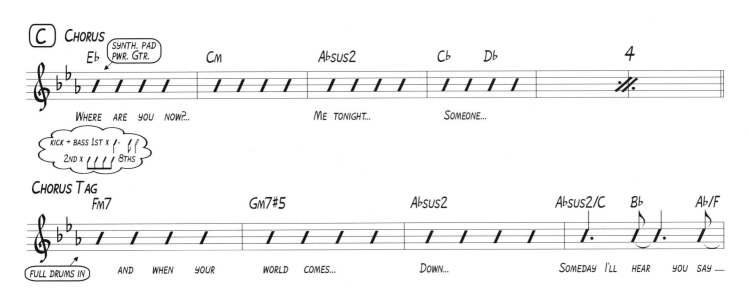

Barry Impresses Brandi with His Lead Sheet

A big eye stared back at Brandi through the peephole.

"Who is it?"

"It's Barry. Remember me? From the beach… You lent me your book…"

"Oh, yeah." The door opened, and Brandi smiled at him. "You came to return my book?"

"Well… no. I kind of lent it to someone. But I'll get it back soon, I promise. I really came to give you the backing track and the lead sheet."

"To what?"

"To the song I wrote for you, remember?"

"Oh… yeah. I didn't think you were really gonna do it. I thought you were just trying to pick up on me."

"Of course not. I'm a serious songwriter… I don't just write songs for anyone though."

"I didn't mean that. I guess you're different from most guys I've met here."

"So… do you wanna hear it?"

"Yeah, sure. Come on in. My tape machine's over there."

"Now let me tell you what I did… I got this guy, Bo, to make a backing track of your song. It's instrumental, because you're singing the lead vocal. I'm going to sing along with the tape right now, so that you can hear the melody."

"*You're* going to sing it? Is this song in my range?"

"Yeah, it's in F. Here's the lead sheet so you can follow along. Don't laugh at my falsetto."

Barry hit "play," closed his eyes, and launched into a spirited rendition of "Surfboard Queen of Idaho." As the final chorus faded, he looked at Brandi. "Well? Whaddya think?"

"You sounded like Michael Jackson in 'Ben.'"

"No. The song. What do you think of the song?"

"I like it. Catchy tune. You were right. It is more me than 'Hard Heart to Break.' I think I'll use it."

"So can I come to your audition and hear my song?"

"Yeah, sure… Why not?"

Epilogue:
Brandi's Second Audition

"Well, Brandi. Welcome back. We hope you're better prepared this time."

"Oh, yes." Her voice echoed from the stage.

"Then talk over your music with Sam."

"This time I have a backing track to sing to. It's an original song."

"Sam, set up Brandi's tape."

Sam looked at Brandi. "No chord chart? Crazy week? No time? Too tough? Give up?"

"No. I just picked a different song."

"Yeah, right."

Sam slipped the cassette into the machine and pressed "play." The first notes of "Surfboard Queen" filled the room, and Brandi took a deep breath. Without missing a beat, she came on strong and didn't let up until the last note. Then silence. It seemed to last forever. Finally...

"Well done, Brandi. Do you have a second number for us?"

"Yes, I do." She dug out her "Hard Heart to Break" chord chart and hesitantly placed it in front of Sam.

"So you *did* use my book."

"Yeah, but I don't know if my chart's any good."

"Well, we'll know real soon, won't we?" He quickly looked it over, then said, "Count it off."

"1...... 2......, 1...2...3...4..." Sam played the intro, and Brandi started singing. She was feeling pretty good by the end of the song.

Sam smiled at her. "Not bad. Not bad at all. You really wailed. You left out a couple of chords in the bridge, but no big deal."

"I can't believe that it worked."

"Good job, Brandi! Be back here, Monday afternoon, two o'clock, soundstage seven. You're on. Good luck! NEXT!"

"Congratulations! See you Monday, Brandi." Sam handed back her chord chart.

"Oh, I almost forgot. Here's your book back. Thanks a lot." She watched the next hopeful take center stage, clutching crumpled sheet music.

Sam followed her eyes. "Maybe you should give it to *him!*"

Form Analysis Chart

Song Title: _____

Songwriter/Artist: _____

Key	Time Signature	Tempo	Melodic Range	Style Description

| Form of Song | | | Road Map Instructions | Comments |
Song Section	Rehearsal Letters	Number of Bars		

Additional Notes:

Common Chord Progressions

The more songs you analyze and transcribe, the easier it will become for you to recognize and identify chords. Below is a list of some common chord progressions. Try playing through each example. If these are fairly easy for you in C major, try playing them in a less familiar key.

Major Progressions

I	vi	ii	V
C	Am	Dm	G

I	vi	IV	V
C	Am	F	G

I	IV	vi	V
C	F	Am	G

I	V	vi	IV
C	G	Am	F

I	IV	V	I
C	F	G	C

I	IV	V	IV
C	F	G	F

I	ii	iii	IV
C	Dm	Em	F

I	iii	IV	V
C	Em	F	G

I	I+	I6	I7	IV	V
C	C+	C6	C7	F	G

I	I+	I6	I7	IV	IV+	IV6
C	C+	C6	C7	F	F+	F6

I	vii7b5	iii7	vi7	ii7	V7
C	B7b5	Em7	Am7	Dm7	G7

I	VII7	III7	VI7	II7	V7
C	B7	E7	A7	D7	G7

I	III7	VI7	II7	V7
C	E7	A7	D7	G7

I	I/bVII	I/VI	bVI
C	C/Bb	C/A	Ab

I	V/VII	vi	I/V	IV	I/III	ii	V7
C	G/B	Am	C/G	F	C/E	Dm	G7

I	I7	IV	iv	I/V	V7	I
C	C7	F	Fm	C/G	G7	C

I	I7	IV	bVII7	I/V	V7	I
C	C7	F	bB7	C/G	G7	C

I	II/I	ii/I	V/I
C	D/C	Dm/C	G/C

I	#I	ii7	V7
C	C#	Dm7	G7

ii	V
Dm	G

IV	V	I
F	G	C

IV	V	vi
F	G	Am

ii7	V7	I	IV	bVII7	III7	vi7 (or VI7)
Dm7	G7	C	F	Bb7	E7	Am7 (or A7)

I	bVII
C	Bb

bVI	bVII	I
Ab	Bb	C

I7	IV7	I7	I7
IV7	IV7	I7	I7
V7	IV7	I7	V7

C7	F7	C7	C7
F7	F7	C7	C7
G7	F7	C7	G7

I	bIII	bV	VI
C	Eb	Gb	A

I	III	#V
C	E	G#

I	II	III	#IV	#V	#VI	I
C	D	E	F#	G#	A#	C

Minor Progressions

i	VII	VI	V
Am	G	F	E

i	i/VII	VI	V
Am	Am/G	F	E

i	i/#VII	i/VII	i/#VI	VI	V
Am	Am/#G	Am/G	Am/#F	F	E

i	i/VII	VI	VII
Am	Am/G	F	G

i	VI	III	VII
Am	F	C	G

i	iv	VI	V
Am	Dm	F	G

i	III	iv	V	VI	VII
Am	C	Dm	E	F	G

i	IV	i	III	IV	i	VII	i
Am	D	Am	C	D	Am	G	Am

i	VII/I	i	VII/I
Am	G/A	Am	G/A

i	VII/I	VI/I	VII/I
Am	G/A	F/A	G/A

The Master Rhythm Chart

When creating charts for rehearsals, demos, recordings, live gigs, etc., many arrangers and copyists will write a separate chord chart for each instrument of the rhythm section plus a lead sheet for the singer. I prefer, however, to write a single comprehensive chart—a master rhythm chart.

A *master rhythm chart*, or composite chart, provides information for both the singer and the band on a single chart. Having piano, guitar, bass, and drums, plus the vocal melody and lyrics, all on one chart allows all the musicians to read from and refer to the same chart. When a rhythm section is playing together, each musician can see what the others are following—if one musician asks a question, the others know what he or she is referring to. They all see the same form, the same number of measures, the same pages.

A drawback to the composite chart is that, if it uses three staffs for every bar of music, the chart is about three times longer than a regular chord chart or lead sheet. It's also definitely not for the beginning copyist-you don't want to attempt a master rhythm chart without first having a few lead sheets and chord charts under your belt.

Included here is a master rhythm chart for the song "Where Are You Now?" Compare this example to the chord chart for the same song in Chapter 11, and use it as a model if you decide to try a master rhythm chart of your own in the future.

MID-TEMPO POP/ROCK BALLAD
WHERE ARE YOU NOW?

WORDS & MUSIC BY ROBIN RANDALL, JUDITHE RANDALL, AND JUNO ROXAS

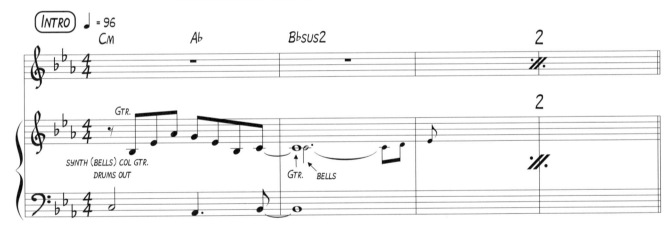

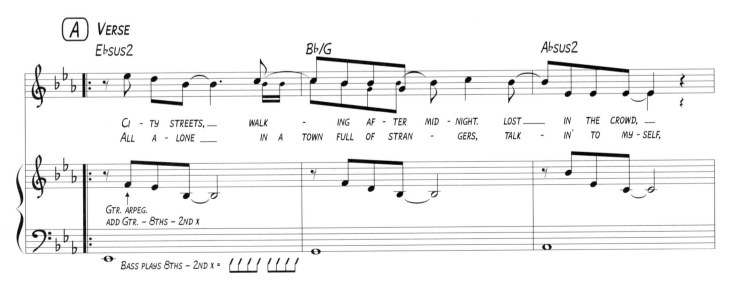

Soulful Pop Ballad
90 **Never Alone**

By Robin Randall, Judithe Randall, James Butler, and Ember Butler

Mid-Tempo Pop/Rock

91 Take It for What It Is

By Robin Randall and Diana DeWitt

INTRO ♩ = 114

Gsus2   Gsus2/B   Csus2   Dsus4 D Dsus2

PIANO

Gsus2   Gsus2/B   Csus2   Dsus4   D

A VERSE

Melody sounds 8vb

Gsus2   Gsus2/E   Gsus2/C

1. It was the first time   might be the on-ly time   so un-ex-pec-ted, caught__
2. A mil-lion miles a-part   can sure-ly break a heart   There is a chance I may nev-

Dsus4   D   Gsus2   Gsus2/E

__ me by sur-prise   I went to say good-bye,   and when your lips touched mine
er see you a-gain.   And if it's meant to be,   __ don't doubt des-tin-y,

Gsus2/C   Dsus4   D   B PRE-CH.   Em

I felt it hap-pen and we __ crossed o-ver, the line. __   We were face to face __
let it take you by __ the hand, don't let it end. __   I am hang-in' on,

A7   Am7   Csus2   D

__ in that far off place __   steal-ing pas-sion in ev' ry hid-ing space __
__ long af-ter you are gone __   what we had was so fat-ed right or wrong.

C CHORUS %

Gsus2   vocal melody as is (loco)   Gsus2/B   Csus2

__ There are no eas-y ans - wers.   There are no prom - is-es

Dsus4 D Dsus2 Gsus2   Gsus2/B   Csus2

no guar-an-teed hap-py end - ings,   just tak it for what __ it __ is

115

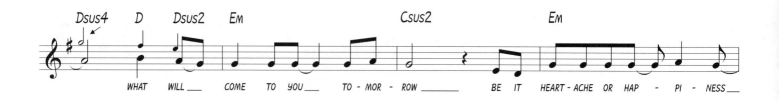

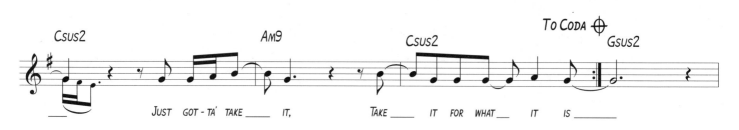

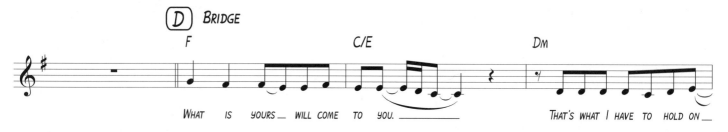

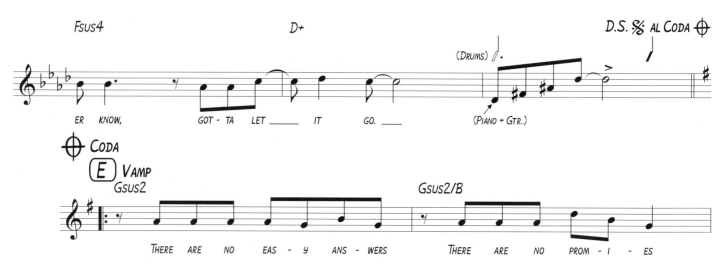

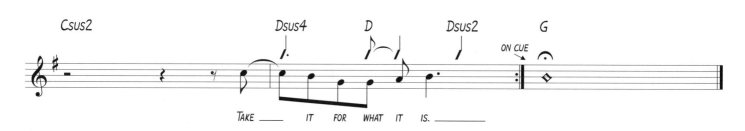

TAKE IT FOR WHAT IT IS

By Robin Randall and Diana DeWitt

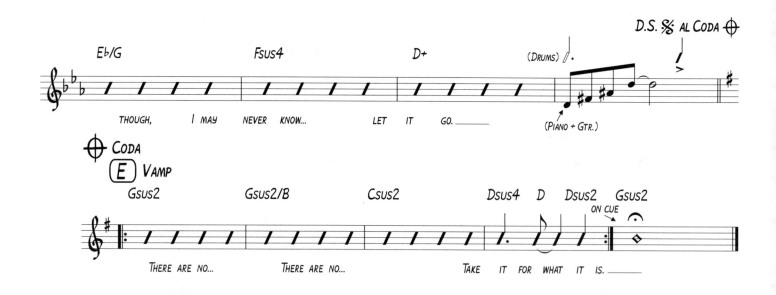

THOUGH, I MAY NEVER KNOW... LET IT GO. _____

Coda

E Vamp

THERE ARE NO... THERE ARE NO... TAKE IT FOR WHAT IT IS. _____

About the Authors

Robin Randall

Robin Randall is an L.A.-based songwriter with a number of hits to her credit, including "Tomorrow Doesn't Matter Tonight" (Starship), "The Last Time" (ABBA's Agnetha Faltskog, produced by Peter Cetera), and "Where Are You Now" (gold #1 single by the Australian band Roxus). Robin's work has also been recorded by the popular British group F.M./U.K., and she is currently under contract as a recording artist with Avex Trax Records (Japan) as one half of Venus & Mars, a duo formed with vocalist/writer Diana De Witt. Recently, Robin and writing partner/mother Judithe Randall have gained worldwide attention for their special montage songs written on assignment for "Baywatch."

Robin is a graduate of the Dick Grove Music School (at which she taught for eight years), and now teaches songwriting, music business, keyboards, and lead sheet writing at Musicians Institute.

Janice Peterson

Janice grew up in Hollywood and now lives in Bozeman, Montana where she and her husband, Dan, own Howler's Inn, a bed and breakfast and wolf sanctuary.

MUSICIANS INSTITUTE

Press

Musicians Institute Press

is the official series of Southern California's renowned music school, Musicians Institute.

MI instructors, some of the finest musicians in the world, share their vast knowledge and experience with you – no matter what your current level. For guitar, bass, drums, vocals, and keyboards, **MI Press** offers the finest music curriculum for higher learning through a variety of series:

FOR MORE INFORMATION, SEE YOUR LOCAL MUSIC DEALER, OR WRITE TO:

HAL•LEONARD®
CORPORATION

7777 W. BLUEMOUND RD. P.O. BOX 13819 MILWAUKEE, WI 53213

ESSENTIAL CONCEPTS

Designed from MI core curriculum programs.

Bass Playing Techniques
by Alexis Sklarevski
00695207 . . . .$14.95

Guitar Improvisation
by Dan Gilbert & Beth Marlis
00695190 . . . .$17.95

Harmony & Theory
by Keith Wyatt & Carl Schroeder
00695161 . . . .$14.95

Music Reading for Guitar
by David Oakes
00695192 . . . .$14.95

Sight Singing
by Mike Campbell
00695195 . . . .$14.95

Music Reading for Bass
by Wendy Wrehovcsik
00695203 . . . .$14.95

Music Reading for Keyboard
by Larry Steelman
00695205 . . . .$14.95

Ear Training
by Keith Wyatt, Carl Schroeder, & Joe Elliot
00695198 . . . .$17.95

Keyboard Voicings
by Kevin King
00695209 . . . .$14.95

Bass Fretboard Basics
by Paul Farnen
00695201 . . . .$14.95

Rhythm Guitar
by Bruce Buckingham & Eric Paschal
00695188 Book/CD $17.95

MASTER CLASS

Designed from MI elective courses.

Rock Lead Basics
by Danny Gill & Nick Nolan
00695144 Book/CD $14.95

Jazz Guitar Improvisation
by Sid Jacobs
00695128 Book/CD $17.95

Jazz Improvisation
by Dave Pozzi
00695135 Book/CD $17.95

Walking Bass
by Bob Magnusson
00695168 Book/CD $17.95

Blues Bass
by Alexis Sklarevski
00695150 Book/CD $17.95

Guitar Playing Techniques
by David Oakes
00695171 . . . .$12.95

Rock Lead Guitar Techniques
by Nick Nolan & Danny Gill
00695146 Book/CD $16.95

PRIVATE LESSONS

Tackle a variety of topics "one-on-one" with MI faculty instructors.

Arpeggios for Bass
by Dave Keif
00695133 . . . .$12.95

Chart Reading for Drummers
00695129 . . . .$19.95

The Diminished Scale for Guitar
by Jean Marc Belkad
00695227 . . . .$7.95

Encyclopedia of Reading Rhythms
by Gary Hess
00695145 Book/CD $19.95

Guitar Basics
by Bruce Buckingham
00695134 Book/CD $14.95

Harmonics for Guitar
by Jamie Findlay
00695169 . . . .$7.95

Lead Sheet Bible
by Robin Randall
00695130 Book/CD $17.95

Modern Approach to Jazz, Rock & Fusion Guitar
by Jean March-Belkadi
00695143 Book/CD $14.95

Odd Meter Bassics
by Dino Monoxelos
00695170 Book/CD $14.95

Open String Chords for Guitar
by Jamie Findlay
00695172 . . . .$7.95

Salsa Hanon
by Peter Deneff
00695226 . . . .$9.95

Working the Inner Clock for Drumset
by Phil Maturano
00695127 . . . .$16.95

Prices, contents, and availability subject to change without notice. Some products may not be available outside of the U.S.A.

0997